Thi

SELECTED RESEARCH
ON
WORK TEAM
DIVERSITY

SELECTED RESEARCH
ON
WORK TEAM
DIVERSITY

Edited by
Marian N. Ruderman
Martha W. Hughes-James
Susan E. Jackson

American Psychological Association
Washington, DC

Center for Creative Leadership
Greensboro, North Carolina

AMERICAN
PSYCHOLOGICAL
ASSOCIATION

750 First Street, NE
Washington, DC 20002

CENTER FOR
CREATIVE
LEADERSHIP

Post Office Box 26300
Greensboro, NC 27438-6300

Library of Congress Cataloging-in-Publication Data

Selected research on work team diversity / edited by Marian N. Ruderman, Martha W. Hughes-James, Susan E. Jackson.
    p. cm.
  Includes bibliographical references.
  ISBN 1-882197-08-9
  1. Diversity in the workplace. 2. Work teams. I. Ruderman, Marian N. II. Hughes-James, Martha W. III. Jackson, Susan E.
HF5549.5.M5D58 1996
331.11'43—dc20

95-34408
CIP

Table of Contents

Foreword

In October 1994 the American Psychological Association, the Center for Creative Leadership, and New York University cosponsored a conference entitled "Work Team Dynamics and Productivity in the Context of Diversity." Its success, judging from participant evaluations, stemmed from the combined strengths of the collaborating organizations. The American Psychological Association, as a preeminent professional association in psychology, has sponsored an important series of meetings (and related volumes) under its Scientific Conferences Program. Contributions from the conference cited above were released in January 1996 by APA Books in the volume *Diversity in Work Teams: Research Paradigms for a Changing Workplace,* and much of the material from the present volume derived from that conference as well. CCL, as an educational institution that conducts both research and training in its own facilities both in the U.S. and abroad, has been successful in bringing together people with different backgrounds and perspectives and providing them with a forum for the exchange of ideas and information. NYU assisted with administrative aspects of the project.

The conference was a means for researchers involved in two important but typically separate areas of organizational concern—workforce diversity and teamwork—and who have widely ranging scientific perspectives and interests (for instance, theory-building, field research, laboratory research) to share information and profit from each other's expertise. Ultimately, this made it possible for everyone to gain a better understanding of the benefits and liabilities of diverse work teams.

We offer this volume in order to broaden the forum that has been established. We hope that it will: (1) inform researchers and practitioners about the current state of knowledge on individual, group, and organizational consequences of work-team diversity; and (2) encourage further research that incorporates the issues of diversity and teams.

We think readers will be impressed by the quality of these papers, which have benefited from the informed feedback of conference attendees.

William C. Howell
Executive Director
Science Directorate
American Psychological Association

Walter W. Tornow
Vice President
Research and Publication
Center for Creative Leadership

Preface

The 1994 conference "Work Team Dynamics and Productivity in the Context of Diversity" featured two types of presentations: invited and submitted papers. The former provided an overview of the emerging field of teams and diversity, and the latter provided important examples of original empirical work that is pushing the field forward.

The best of the submitted papers are featured in this volume. We are pleased to make these available to a wider audience. The papers prepared by invited participants are published in *Diversity in Work Teams: Research Paradigms for a Changing Workplace* (American Psychological Association, 1995).

We would like to take this opportunity to thank the conference sponsors: the American Psychological Association, the Center for Creative Leadership, and New York University. Donations from several corporations also helped make the conference possible: BancOne Corporation; Philip Morris Companies, Inc.; Pfizer Inc.; and Sara Lee Knit Products (a division of Sara Lee Corporation). Walt Tornow deserves special mention for his encouragement and support during the planning of the event. We especially thank all of the conference participants, who shared their wealth of knowledge on diversity and teams research, generated stimulating discussion, and provided feedback and insights for the authors of these papers.

In addition, we owe much gratitude to Patti Hall for managing the multitude of details that made the conference a success. We also appreciate other Center staff who generously gave of their time and effort in shaping and implementing the conference: Karen Boylston, Karen McNeil-Miller, Debbie Nelson, Luke Novelli, John Sayres, Valerie Sessa, and Walt Tornow.

Finally, we thank the people who helped with the preparation of this volume. Debbie Nelson provided administrative support throughout the various stages of revisions. Marcia Horowitz and Martin Wilcox gave invaluable editorial support. Joanne Ferguson designed and proofread the manuscript. And, of course, we acknowledge the authors of these seven papers for their contribution to the generation of knowledge on diversity and teams.

Introduction

Marian N. Ruderman
Martha W. Hughes-James
Susan E. Jackson

Understanding the dynamics of diverse teams is increasingly important in today's world. More than ever before, organizations are relying on teams as a way to increase productivity (Jackson & Alvarez, 1992). At the same time that teams are becoming more prominent, organizations are growing more diverse (Johnston & Packer, 1987). While they have always been a strong presence in the American workforce, white women, women of color, and men of color are reaching higher organizational levels and achieving in occupations from which they have traditionally been excluded. Also, American companies are becoming more global in orientation (Kanter, 1991).

Research on the dynamics of diverse work teams is a relatively new area of inquiry in organizational psychology. Although there is a long history of research on teams and a growing field regarding diversity, relatively few studies have been conducted on diverse teams. The accumulated knowledge to date, however, suggests an intriguing pattern of findings about the effects of group composition on team outcomes. On the one hand, diversity in teams is associated with innovation and problem solving stemming from the multiplicity of perspectives available. On the other, it is associated with low levels of group integration and higher turnover stemming in part from in-group biases, stereotyping, and clashing perspectives. In other words, diversity in the context of work teams has both benefits and liabilities. This literature is sparse, however, with only a few studies providing insights into the effects of diversity due to race, ethnicity, and gender (for reviews of relevant literature, see Cox, 1993; Jackson, May, & Whitney, 1995; Jackson & Ruderman, 1995; Nemeth, 1986).

This book contains seven papers from a conference on diversity and teams held at the Center in October 1994. The authors examine diversity in terms of a variety of attributes, with several papers looking at heterogeneity in terms of race and sex. By making this information more accessible, we hope to stimulate new research, which can eventually be used to guide organizations as they wrestle with the challenge of managing diversity effectively.

Because it presents some of the most recent research on the topic of diversity within teams, this volume should be of particular interest to social scientists and students interested in studying the issue of workforce diversity. Although it does not attempt to provide direct advice about how to manage diversity within the context of the workplace, practitioners may nevertheless find that this book enriches their understanding of the dynamics of diversity.

These works should be regarded as exploratory research. This is a relatively young field and one without a dominant paradigm or methodology. Each of the six empirical papers and the one conceptual paper attempts to further this area of inquiry. They use a variety of samples, research methodologies, and ways of assessing diversity. These studies are not without their limitations; this is a difficult area of inquiry where it is hard to "control" variables or conduct manipulations. Furthermore, the field studies take place in organizations where there is little attention to diversity. None of the organizations studied prepared their teams to deal with their own diversity. This lack of attention to settings supportive of diversity is an important caveat in interpreting the findings of the field studies and has implications for further development in this area of inquiry. Despite these limitations, these papers represent what is known and are valuable as a point for charting further avenues of science and practice.

The book is divided into three sections. The first deals with the management of diverse groups. These three papers offer empirical treatments of what the experience of managing a diverse team is like and what needs to be taken into account in developing such teams. The second section focuses on empirical assessment of the impact of team composition on group processes and outputs. These three studies take place in organizations where diversity has been largely unattended to. The one paper in the third section offers a theoretical treatment of the issues involved in enhancing the processes of diverse work teams.

Management of diverse teams. In this section, Mayo, Meindl, and Pastor focus our attention on leaders of diverse teams. The authors compare the perceptions of leaders of single-sex groups to those of mixed-sex groups. Laboratory methods are used to understand the effects of diversity on leaders' self-perceptions and perceptions of their work group. The results indicate that leaders of heterogeneous groups perceived the work group and themselves more negatively than did the leaders of homogeneous groups, suggesting that leading gender-heterogeneous groups is more taxing than leading gender-homogeneous groups.

The next paper, by James, Chen, and Cropanzano, deals with leadership in multinational organizations. This study investigates leadership values and expectations for leadership among workers in Taiwan and the United States. The results suggest that these two groups have different implicit theories of leadership, which stem from different cultural values. This study illustrates the importance of examining how national culture shapes leadership activities and organizational policies. In their conclusions, the authors suggest that effective management of multicultural organizations may require adopting leadership activities that are tailored to match the differing cultural perspectives of employees.

Leader values and expectations also are explored by Gelfand, Kuhn, and Radhakrishnan, who offer a theoretical model for understanding value similarities and differences between employees and supervisors. These authors posit that value differences shape social-interaction processes, which in turn affect job-related outcomes. Data from employee-supervisor pairs from a large U.S.-based organization are used to test the hypothesized model, and considerable support for the model is found. Similarity of values is associated with communication processes, and communication is associated with job-related outcomes such as job satisfaction and organizational withdrawal. Employees who share similar values with their supervisors are more likely to be satisfied with their job and less likely to withdraw from work.

The impact of group composition. These papers empirically examine the impact of group composition on a variety of outcomes. First, Eigel and Kuhnert consider the impact of personality diversity on social interactions and productivity for teams of sales managers in a retail organization. In the strongly monocultural company they studied, diversity of personalities was associated with lower productivity. The authors suggest that this relationship is a function of the value put on being a particular personality type and the homogeneity that results from this emphasis.

In the next paper, DiTomaso, Cordero, and Farris describe the effects of group diversity on perceptions of group and self. Using a U.S. sample of scientists and engineers from twenty-four industries, they examined the relationship between work-group diversity and three outcomes: (1) perceptions of group process; (2) individual perceptions of career opportunities; and (3) the well-being of group members. Their focus is on understanding the impact of group cohesiveness on feelings about the group and one's place in it. Their evidence suggests that being in low-status or minority positions is associated with psychological discomfort. These effects appear to be mediated by other aspects of the relationship between self and the group, however. The authors argue that these effects are more problematic in work groups that have not developed norms for effective teamwork.

The next paper focuses on the relationship between work-group composition and diversity climate. Using longitudinal data, Kossek, Zonia, and Young investigate the relationship between work-group demography and employee attitudes and behaviors regarding diversity. The study was conducted in an organization that actively recruited white women, women of color, and men of color but then did little to facilitate their integration into work units. The findings suggest that increasing organizational diversity is not enough to change organizational attitudes toward diversity. Organizations may need to couple recruiting efforts with group-process and structural-change efforts in order to bring about the advantages of diversity.

The dynamics of group process. In the one paper in this section, Raghuram and Garud offer a theoretical framework for understanding interpersonal processes within diverse groups. They use a process perspective to analyze when diversity leads to increased team productivity and when it results in conflict and dissatisfaction. The authors argue that several mechanisms drive a group's process over time and that understanding these mechanisms can lead to improved group functioning. The basic premise is that it is essential to understand the processes of diverse teams in order to reap the benefits of diversity.

Together, these papers emphasize the importance of studying team dynamics in the context of diversity. They highlight the importance of concepts such as transformational leadership, cultural values, communication processes, group composition, psychological well-being, and climate for diversity. As a collection, these works show there is great value in understanding the impact of diversity on team functioning.

References

Cox, T. H. (1993). *Cultural diversity in organizations.* San Francisco: Berrett-Koehler.

Jackson, S. E., & Alvarez, E. B. (1992). Working through diversity as a strategic imperative. In S. E. Jackson (Ed.), *Diversity in the workplace: Human resources initiatives.* New York: Guilford Press.

Jackson, S. E., & Ruderman, M. N. (Eds.). (1995). *Diversity in work teams: Research paradigms for a changing workplace.* Washington, DC: American Psychological Association.

Jackson, S. E., May, K. A., & Whitney, K. (1995). Understanding the dynamics of diversity in decision making teams. In R. A. Guzzo & E. Salas (Eds.), *Team decision making effectiveness in organizations*. San Francisco: Jossey-Bass.

Johnston, W. B., & Packer, A. E. (1987). *Workforce 2000: Work and workers for the 21st century*. Washington, DC: U.S. Department of Labor.

Kanter, R. M. (May-June, 1991). Transcending business boundaries: 12,000 world managers view change. *Harvard Business Review*, pp. 151-164.

Nemeth, C. J. (1986). Differential contributions of majority and minority influence. *Psychological Review, 91*, 23-32.

THE MANAGEMENT OF
DIVERSE TEAMS

THE COST OF LEADING DIVERSITY: EFFECTS OF GROUP DIVERSITY ON LEADERS' PERCEPTIONS

Margarita C. Mayo
James R. Meindl
Juan-Carlos Pastor

School of Management
State University of New York at Buffalo

Abstract

In an earlier study, Mayo, Meindl, and Pastor (1994) investigated the effects of group diversity on followers' perceptions of their leaders. This study goes a step further and examines the effects of group diversity on leaders' perceptions of their work groups and themselves. Two general research questions were addressed: (1) Do leaders of heterogeneous groups perceive their work groups more negatively than leaders of homogeneous groups? and (2) Do leaders of heterogeneous groups perceive themselves more negatively than leaders of homogeneous groups? Data were collected about leaders' perceptions on several leadership dimensions and group dynamics. The study found that leaders of heterogeneous groups perceive the work group and themselves more negatively. Comparisons with the earlier study on followers are made, and implications for the results of this study are suggested.

⁂ ⁂ ⁂

Diversity has become a fact of life for many organizations. The growing service economy, globalization, and the changing nature of the workforce have contributed to increased diversity in the workplace (Jackson & Alvarez, 1992; Kotter, 1985). At the same time, organizations are more likely to arrange work around teams (Walton & Hackman, 1986). For example, many

---

This research was supported by an endowment from Marine Midland.

organizations are implementing total quality management programs that emphasize teamwork (Dean & Bowen, 1994).

At the core of this teamwork is leadership. Most work teams are formally managed by an appointed or formal leader. Even self-managed teams are likely to experience leadership as role differentiation develops and one or more members emerge as informal leader(s) (Bass, 1990). Leadership is also considered one of the most critical factors in the success or failure of work units (Bass, 1990). Together, the trends of a diverse workforce and more work being done in teams are bringing more leaders to manage demographically diverse groups.

The management of diverse groups may put additional demands and challenges on leaders in several ways. Research has shown that the demographic composition of the group has an important effect on how group members feel and behave. For example, O'Reilly, Caldwell, and Barnett (1989) found that members of diverse groups experience more negative feelings toward other group members, and that individuals most different from others on demographic attributes were the least socially integrated into the group and the most likely to exit. Similarly, group diversity may have a powerful effect on how leaders feel, think, and behave. Thus, the study of the relationship between group diversity and leadership is of both theoretical and practical significance.

Several authors have also pointed out that the size of groups is likely to affect what the leader does and thinks (see also Bass, 1990). For example, Goodstadt and Kipnis (1970) found that as group size increased, supervisors tended to spend less time with poor workers and to give fewer pay raises to good workers. Also, Hemphill (1950) found that as the size of the groups increased, the members made greater demands on the leaders. Larger groups made significantly stronger demands on the leaders' strength, reliability, and coordination.

Group heterogeneity may be another important characteristic of the group affecting leaders, because homogeneous and heterogeneous groups are likely to put different responsibilities and demands on them. Though previous studies have investigated the effects of group heterogeneity on group members, there is a lack of studies that examine the impact of group heterogeneity on leaders. This study took a step in that direction by examining the effects of gender heterogeneity on leaders' perceptions of their work groups and themselves. The study of leaders' perceptions is important because leaders behave in accord with the context they have perceived (Bass, 1990). Examination of leaders' perceptions in the context of diversity will provide valuable knowledge to understand their behaviors and, eventually, to help them to be more effective when managing diverse groups.

In an earlier study (Mayo, Meindl, & Pastor, 1994), we investigated the effects of group diversity on followers' perceptions of their leaders. By using an experimental design, we examined how followers' perceptions of the charismatic and transactional qualities of their leaders varied with group heterogeneity. We found that members of heterogeneous groups perceived their emergent leaders as more charismatically appealing than members of homogeneous groups. However, there was no evidence of significant differences between members of heterogeneous and homogeneous groups on their perceptions of transactional leadership attributes. As part of this study, we collected data about leaders' perceptions on several leadership dimensions and group dynamics. This study focused on the leaders' responses and addresses two general research questions: (1) Do leaders of heterogeneous groups perceive their work groups more negatively than leaders of homogeneous groups? and (2) Do leaders of heterogeneous groups perceive themselves more negatively than leaders of homogeneous groups?

Theoretical Overview

The general research questions are divided into seven specific questions, according to generally understood concepts in the literature.

Leaders' Perceptions of Their Work Groups

Some of the most important aspects of group dynamics are social cohesion and group climate (Forsyth, 1990).

Social cohesion. Social cohesion is a key concept for the understanding of group processes. It refers to each member's attraction to other group members or to "the degree to which the members of the group desire to remain in their group" (Cartwright, 1968, p. 91). Byrne's (1971) similarity-attraction paradigm suggests that similarities in demographic attributes such as sex, age, race, and tenure lead group members to infer that other group members share their attitudes, values, and beliefs, increasing their feelings of security. In contrast, dissimilarity in these attributes may lead group members to infer that other group members have different attitudes and values, increasing their feelings of distrust, discomfort, and fear. Based on this paradigm, several studies have shown that heterogeneous groups are likely to be less cohesive than homogeneous groups (Lott & Lott, 1965; O'Reilly, Caldwell,

& Barnett, 1989). In turn, this lack of cohesion results in high turnover rates. Empirical evidence indicates that group heterogeneity in terms of age is related to turnover in academic units (McCain, O'Reilly, & Pfeffer, 1983), in top-management teams (Jackson, Brett, Sessa, Cooper, Julin, & Peyronnin, 1991; Wagner, Pfeffer, & O'Reilly, 1984), and among nurses in hospitals (Pfeffer & O'Reilly, 1987). Thus, significant evidence supports the notion that heterogeneous groups are less socially integrated, as perceived by group members. Similarly, it could be expected that leaders of heterogeneous groups would be aware of this lack of cohesion.

> *Question 1.* Is there a relationship between group heterogeneity and leaders' perception of the group's social cohesion? More specifically, do leaders of heterogeneous groups report that their work groups are less cohesive than leaders of homogeneous groups?

Group climate. Group climate refers to the type of emotional atmosphere that describes the teamwork (e.g., James & Jones, 1974). Diversity is often associated with prejudice and stereotyping, creating emotions of hostility and discomfort among members of heterogeneous groups (Devine, Monteith, Zuwerink, & Elliot, 1991; Jackson, May, & Whitney, 1995; Morrison, 1992). For example, members of heterogeneous groups have been found to experience feelings of dislike (O'Reilly et al., 1989; Rosenbaum, 1986), having low frequency of communication (Lincoln & Miller, 1979), and to be less psychologically committed to the organization (Tsui, Egan, & O'Reilly, 1992). These feelings are likely to create a negative climate in the work group which would be perceived by the leader.

> *Question 2.* Is there a relationship between group heterogeneity and leaders' perception of the group's climate? Do leaders of heterogeneous groups perceive their work groups as having a more negative climate than leaders of homogeneous groups?

Self-perception of Leadership

In this section we examine the effects of group heterogeneity on several aspects of self-perception of leadership, namely leadership styles—transactional and transformational leadership—and leaders' effectiveness, happiness, role ambiguity, and influencing behavior.

Transactional and transformational leadership. Recent developments in the area of leadership have emphasized two forms of leadership, namely transactional and transformational leadership (Bass, 1985, 1990; Burns, 1978). Transactional leadership refers to a relationship between leaders and followers characterized by exchange processes in which leaders satisfy followers' needs and followers comply with the demands of their leaders. In this exchange process, both leaders and followers perceive each other as being potentially instrumental to each other's goals and needs such as when they are jointly engaged in accomplishment of a task (Bass, 1990).

In contrast, transformational leadership refers to a relationship between leaders and followers by which both leaders and followers transcend their own personal interests to the benefit of higher order values and principles (Burns, 1978). During the transformational process leaders are viewed as visionary, charismatic, sensitive to individuals' needs and feelings, and inspirational (e.g., Bass, 1985; Burns, 1978; Conger, 1989; Conger & Kanungo, 1988). Charisma has been found to be the major component of transformational leadership (Bass, 1985). Charismatic relationships are characterized by followers' intense emotional feelings about their leaders, unquestioning acceptance of their leaders' beliefs, and emotional attachment to the mission. The two forms of leadership are not mutually exclusive. Rather, the same individuals are likely to display charismatic and transactional leadership with different frequency (Bass, 1985).

As Jackson (1991) has pointed out, diversity has changed the patterns of behavior established during a time when work groups were relatively homogeneous. These changes have created a number of interpersonal challenges for groups, such as intragroup conflict (Kotter, 1985) and communication barriers (Graves & Powell, 1994). Leaders of heterogeneous groups may not have the strategies of action needed to deal with these new challenges, leaving them with feelings of a lack of accomplishment and self-blame. The leadership literature suggests that leaders are more likely than others to be held responsible for group processes and outcomes (Hollander, 1978; Meindl, 1990). For example, Farris and Lim (1969) found that leaders whose accession to office coincides with a group failure will earn members' blame for it. Similarly, Meindl (1990) and his colleagues found that leaders were blamed for rather mild mistakes, even when the responsibility for the mistake was shared with co-workers. In the same vein, leaders may see themselves in the same way as others see them. For instance, self-perception theory maintains that people's perceptions of their own behaviors are similar to the perceptions of others (Bem, 1972; Ryle, 1949). Accordingly, it is reasonable to expect that leaders themselves would tend to accept responsibility and would blame themselves for difficulties associated with the work group. Leaders of heterogeneous groups may blame themselves for the challenges associated with diversity, resulting in more negative views of themselves as leaders than those dealing with more homogeneous teams. In particular, they may be more likely to evaluate themselves low on important leadership dimensions such as charismatic and transactional leadership.

> *Question 3.* Is there a relationship between group heterogeneity and leaders' self-perception of charismatic and transactional leadership? Do leaders of heterogeneous groups evaluate themselves lower on charismatic and transactional attributes than leaders of homogeneous groups?

Leader effectiveness. The literature on effective leadership has emphasized the study of outcome measures, such as satisfaction, extra effort, motivation, and commitment (Bass, 1990). This research has mainly focused on subordinates' outcomes rather than leaders' outcomes. It has examined the degree to which subordinates consider the leader effective, the level to which subordinates are satisfied with the leader, and are motivated and willing to exert extra effort (see also Bass, 1990). However, less attention has been paid to the extent to which leaders perceive themselves to be effective, motivated in the task, satisfied, and committed to the team. It is possible that, because of the different responsibilities and demands that work groups put on leaders, their own level of effectiveness, satisfaction, motivation, and commitment varies with the level of heterogeneity of the group.

> *Question 4.* Is there a relationship between group heterogeneity and leaders' evaluations of leadership effectiveness? Do leaders of heterogeneous groups report lower ratings on leadership effectiveness than leaders of homogeneous groups?

Happiness. Because leaders are thought of as having more influence over other group members, more control over group processes and outcomes, greater visibility, and greater responsibility for failures (Hollander, 1978), leaders of heterogeneous groups may tend to blame themselves for some of the difficulties associated with group diversity. This process of self-blame may reduce leaders' sense of self-efficacy as leaders and result in a negative emotional state. Accordingly, leaders of heterogeneous groups may experience feelings of sadness and unhappiness to a greater extent than leaders of homogeneous groups.

Question 5. Is there a relationship between group heterogeneity and leaders' feelings? Do leaders of heterogeneous groups feel less happy than leaders of homogeneous groups?

Role ambiguity. Role ambiguity occurs when work objectives are unclear and the demands of several tasks are incompatible (Ivancevich & Matteson, 1980). Leaders may also experience role ambiguity when they cannot meet the interpersonal demands of their role (Bass, 1990). Because diversity is associated with change (Jackson, 1991), leaders of heterogeneous groups may be more likely to experience higher levels of uncertainty and ambiguity. These leaders may experience more difficulties in predicting the behaviors of their group members and in establishing standards against which to evaluate the appropriate social behavior of group members.

Question 6. Is there a relationship between group heterogeneity and leaders' role ambiguity? Do leaders of heterogeneous groups experience higher levels of role ambiguity than leaders of homogeneous groups?

Influence tactics. One of the most important determinants of leader effectiveness is success in influencing subordinates (Yukl, 1994). Leaders carry out active tactics of influence with the intention of changing the minds of their followers (Falbe & Yukl, 1992; Yukl & Falbe, 1990; Yukl, Falbe, & Joo, 1993; Yukl & Tracey, 1992). Yukl and Falbe's (1990) classification of nine influence tactics will be used in this research because it is consistent with the new advances on charismatic and participative leadership. These nine tactics are commonly organized into three broader categories (Falbe & Yukl, 1992): (1) Hard-influence tactics include legitimating tactics and pressure tactics and some forms of coalition and exchange tactics; these tactics tend to be used in distant and controlling ways. (2) Soft-influence tactics include inspirational appeal, consultation, ingratiation, and personal appeals; these tactics tend to be used in personal and polite ways. (3) Rational tactics involve the use of logical arguments and include rational persuasion tactics.[†] Research on influence tactics suggests that people who use forceful, demanding, and hard tactics are disliked (French & Raven, 1959) and have less

---

[†]In this study we do not include legitimate tactics because the emergent leaders of this study did not have any positional or legitimate power. We include rational tactics as a type of soft tactic since the use of logical arguments may also be seen as a polite way to influence subordinates.

influence over their targets (Yukl & Tracey, 1992). Given that heterogeneous groups face more interpersonal challenges than homogeneous groups (e.g., O'Reilly et al., 1989), leaders of heterogeneous groups may more strongly avoid the use of persistent and demanding tactics and may be more likely to influence followers with polite and soft tactics.

> *Question 7.* Is there a relationship between group heterogeneity and leaders' report of influence tactics? Do leaders of heterogeneous groups report lower levels of hard tactics and greater levels of soft tactics than leaders of homogeneous groups?

Method

Although a laboratory study may have limitations in terms of the generalizability of the results, the following reasons led us to believe that an experimental design was the most appropriate methodology to examine these research questions. This study is the first attempt to understand the relationship between group heterogeneity and leaders' perceptions, and we wanted to examine if the expected effects appear under controlled conditions before testing it in the field. We systematically varied the degree of group heterogeneity while keeping other characteristics of the groups such as task and setting as similar as possible. This experimental design allowed us to control for other group characteristics such as group tenure and educational and age group heterogeneity, thereby increasing the internal validity of the study. Finally, the treatment (degree of gender heterogeneity) can be easily manipulated within an experimental design.

Sample

A total of 125 undergraduate students (30 groups of 3 to 6 people each) from introductory business classes at a large Northeastern university volunteered to participate in the study. Sixty females and 65 males participated in partial fulfillment of course requirements. The average age of the participants was 22 years; most (80%) were non-minorities, and about half (58%) had work experience. Out of the 125 participants, 30 were selected as leaders by their group members. These 30 emergent leaders comprise the sample for this study which includes 15 females and 15 males.

Procedure

The gender composition of the group was manipulated to create three diversity conditions: (1) homogeneous groups (either male homogeneous or female homogeneous), (2) low-heterogeneity groups (minority male or minority female), and (3) high-heterogeneity groups (half female and half male). The procedure involves five steps, namely introduction to the experiment, leaderless discussion session, choosing a group leader, working on a group reaction paper with the emergent leader, and an individual paper-and-pencil questionnaire. All the steps were conducted in one continuous session, which took approximately one hour.

Introduction: Participants were first greeted by a female experimenter who verified their names and explained the nature of the study:

> We're interested in knowing about the nature of the sexual-harassment problem on campus and about how undergraduates work together to solve and prevent this problem. In this study you will be part of a group of people who will be asked to discuss, for 10 minutes, the problem of sexual harassment on campus, then you will have to choose a leader who will guide and coordinate the next 10 minutes in which the group has to write a "reaction paper" on what kind of actions could be taken to help prevent future cases of sexual harassment. After 10 minutes of teamwork, members of the group will be asked to fill out some questions about the dynamics of the group.

Prior to their participation, subjects were asked to read and sign an informed consent form and were given the option to terminate their participation without penalty.

Leaderless discussion session: The discussion session was designed to familiarize subjects with each other and to provide them with personal information on which to base their judgments for choosing a leader. Because this study was the first attempt to examine the effects of gender heterogeneity on leaders, we reasoned that a structural variable such as gender heterogeneity would have more influence on leaders' perceptions as they become aware of it. Thus, we expected that a gender-related task such as discussing the topic of sexual harassment would make leaders more aware of the level of gender heterogeneity in the group. Subjects first read a short essay with some examples of sexual harassment on campus. They were then instructed to discuss, for 10 minutes, the general topic of sexual harassment. A video camera randomly recorded some of the discussion sessions.

Choosing a group leader: Afterwards, subjects were asked to choose a leader who would guide and coordinate the teamwork in the next session. They did so, first individually, ranking each member of the group in order of preference; and second as a group, arriving at consensus about who the leader of the group would be for the teamwork session.

A teamwork session: The teamwork session was designed to provide participants with a real situation in which they could evaluate their emergent leader. As a group with its emergent leader, subjects were asked to compose, in 10 minutes, a reaction paper on the issue of sexual harassment on campus. The leader of each group received a sheet of blank paper on which they wrote their thoughts. The leader's assignment was to coordinate the task by promoting group discussion, organizing ideas, and helping to decide what should be written in the reaction paper.

Paper-and-pencil questionnaires: Finally, each member of the group, including the leader, completed a questionnaire which contained all dependent measures. Before leaving, subjects were debriefed by the experimenter.

Measures

This study examines the effects of group heterogeneity on leaders' perceptions of several aspects of group dynamics and leadership. This section describes the measures used to assess leaders' perceptions.

Group heterogeneity. Leaders were assigned diversity scores as a function of their membership in homogeneous, low-heterogeneous, and high-heterogeneous groups. Since there was not much difference in the size of the groups, we decided to assign 0, 1, and 2 for membership to homogeneous, low-heterogeneous, and high-heterogeneous groups, respectively.

Social cohesion. Two items used by O'Reilly et al. (1989) were used to assess leaders' perceptions of social cohesion: "How well did members of our group stick together?" ranging from 1 = great, couldn't be better, to 5 = not very good; and "To what extent would members be ready to defend each other from criticism by outsiders?" ranging from 1 = not at all to 5 = very much (Cronbach alpha = .77).

Group climate. Leaders' evaluations of group climate were measured by use of 7 pairs of adjectives describing the climate of the group during the group discussion and teamwork. For example, pessimistic vs. optimistic, boring vs. fun, and tedious vs. stimulating. Pairs of adjectives were evaluated on a 7-point scale format ranging from 1 = negative climate to 7 = positive climate (Cronbach alpha = .84).

Charismatic (transformational) leadership. Evaluations of one's own charisma were measured by use of a questionnaire including items from 3 different sources: (1) the charisma scale from the Multifactor Leadership Questionnaire (Bass & Avolio, 1990; e.g., "I make others feel good around me"); (2) 4 items of charisma developed by Shamir (1992; e.g., "I am an energetic and dynamic person"); and (3) 13 items created for this study based on Conger's (1989) behavioral description of charismatic leaders (e.g., "I use metaphors and stories when communicating with other members of the group"). In addition, a single general item of charisma was included: "I am charismatic." All items were evaluated on a 5-point scale format, ranging from 1 = totally disagree to 5 = totally agree (Cronbach alpha = .80).

Transactional leadership. Evaluations of transactional leadership were measured via the contingent-reward and management-by-exception scales from the Multifactor Leadership Questionnaire (Bass & Avolio, 1990). An example of a contingent reward item is: "I give others recognition when they have a good idea." All items were evaluated on a 5-point scale format, ranging from 1 = totally disagree to 5 = totally agree (Cronbach alpha for contingent reward = .76). The reliability for management-by-exception scale was not acceptable; thus, it was not used in the analyses.

Leadership effectiveness. This included 4 items: "How effective were you working as the leader of the group?"; "How motivated were you working on the task?"; "How satisfied are you with the teamwork?"; and "How committed are you to the group?" All items ranged from 1 = not at all to 5 = very much (Cronbach alpha = .75).

Happiness. A single pair of adjectives, namely sad vs. happy, evaluated leaders' emotional state. Leaders evaluated how they felt being the leader of the group on a 5-point scale from sad to happy.

Role ambiguity. Two new items were created for this study which included: "To what extent did you know the behaviors that were appropriate and acceptable in the group?" and "How well could you predict the reactions and behaviors of the other members of the group?" Both items ranged from 1 = not at all to 5 = very much (Cronbach alpha = .70).

Influence tactics. This included 8 items based on Yukl and Tracey's (1992) description of 8 influence tactics: rational, inspirational, consultation, ingratiation, exchange, personal appeal, others' support, and pressure tactics. The first 5 items measure soft tactics. An example of soft tactics is: "I make a request or proposal that arouses enthusiasm by appealing to their values, ideals, and confidence." The other 3 items measure hard tactics. An example of hard tactics is: "I use demands or threats to influence them to do what I want." All items were evaluated on a 5-point scale format ranging from 1 = I never use this tactic to 5 = I use this tactic very often (Cronbach alpha is .69 for soft tactics and .68 for hard tactics).

Results

Descriptive Statistics

The means, standard deviations, reliabilities, and correlations among the variables are shown in Table 1. The scales showed satisfactory reliabilities, as measured with Cronbach alpha. A frequency analysis of the number of times men and women emerged as leaders in heterogeneous groups showed that: (1) In low-heterogeneous groups, neither token women nor token men were selected as leaders of their groups; and (2) in high-heterogeneous groups, women and men became the leader of their groups the same number of times (5 female and 5 male).

Leaders' Perceptions of Their Work Groups

Question 1. To test the idea that leaders of heterogeneous groups perceive their work groups as less socially integrated than leaders of homogeneous groups, we computed a bivariate correlation between group heterogeneity and leaders' reports of group cohesion. The results showed that there was a statistically significant negative correlation between diversity and social cohesion ($r = -.30$, $p < .05$), indicating that leaders of heterogeneous groups perceive their group members as less socially integrated than leaders of homogeneous groups.

Question 2. To examine the notion that leaders of heterogeneous groups perceive the emotional climate of their group more negatively than leaders of homogeneous groups, we computed bivariate correlations between group heterogeneity and leaders' reports of group climate. The findings indicate that there is a marginally significant negative correlation between gender heterogeneity and group climate ($r = -.20$, $p < .10$). The tedious vs. stimulating dimension of group climate showed the highest negative correlation with diversity ($r = -.32$, $p < .05$). These results suggest that leaders of heterogeneous groups perceive their groups as having a more negative emotional climate than leaders of homogeneous groups. Particularly, leaders of heterogeneous groups are more likely than leaders of homogeneous groups to find the group climate tedious rather than stimulating.

Table 1. Means, Standard Deviations, Reliabilities, and Correlation Coefficients Among Variables

Variables	M	SD	1	2	3	4	5	6	7	8	9	10
1. Group heterogeneity	—	—	—	-.05	-.18	-.31*	-.39**	-.02	-.20	-.30*	.30*	-.46**
2. Charismatic leadership	3.60	.30		(.80)	.60**	.27	.35*	.75**	.30*	.06	-.29	.55**
3. Transactional leadership	3.74	.40			(.76)	.43*	.51**	.43**	.10	.06	-.35*	.36*
4. Leadership effectiveness	3.94	.68				(.75)	.20	.40**	.41**	.30*	-.17	.31*
5. Hard-influence tactics	2.66	.89					(.68)	.43**	.25	.21	-.40**	.35*
6. Soft-influence tactics	4.04	.69						(.69)	.46**	.28	-.35*	.30
7. Group climate	5.74	.93							(.84)	.54**	-.04	.24
8. Social cohesion	3.98	.70								(.77)	.11	.09
9. Role ambiguity	2.62	.70									(.70)	-.40**
10. Happiness	4.14	.82										—

$N = 30$ leaders.   * $p < .05$, ** $p < .01$
Reliability coefficients are in parentheses

Self-perception of Leadership

Question 3. To examine the idea that leaders of heterogeneous groups evaluate themselves lower on charismatic and transactional attributes, we first computed bivariate correlations between group heterogeneity and leaders' self-perceptions of transactional and charismatic leadership. Correlation analyses indicated that there was a marginally significant correlation between diversity and leaders' self-perceptions of transactional leadership attributes ($r = -.18, p < .10$). However, there was no evidence of a statistically significant relationship between diversity and leaders' self-perception of charismatic attributes. Although the results of the correlation analyses were suggestive, discriminant analysis was used as a more sophisticated way to examine the relationship between group heterogeneity and leaders' perceptions of leadership. A stepwise discriminant analysis minimizing residuals on 25 leadership items was used (14 charismatic items and 11 transactional items). We also tested the efficiency of this set of discriminating items in correctly classifying the leaders in the 3 experimental conditions over random probability. The leadership items were used as predictor variables and the level of group diversity as the criterion variable. The grouping variable had 3 categories— leaders of homogeneous, low-heterogeneous, and high-heterogeneous groups—with sample sizes of 10 in each group. The prior probabilities for the classification analysis were .33 for each group.

The discriminant analysis revealed a best set of discriminating factors that consisted of 8 items (4 charismatic and 4 transactional) and yielded 2 functions that were statistically significant. The first function had an eigenvalue of 1.45, accounted for 62.92% of the between-group variance, and had a canonical correlation of .77, Wilks's $\Lambda = .22$, $\chi^2 = 35.67$ ($df = 16, n = 30$, $p < .003$). The second function had an eigenvalue of .85, accounted for the remaining 37.08% of the between-group variance, and had a canonical correlation of .68, Wilks's $\Lambda = .54$, $\chi^2 = 14.55$ ($df = 7, n = 30, p < .04$). Table 2 includes the standardized canonical discriminant weights for each function.

An examination of the magnitude of the standardized coefficients (ignoring the sign) tells us about the relative contribution of the item to determining scores on the function (Klecka, 1980; Tatsuoka, 1988). The first function is best defined by high weights on items 9, 18, and 26. Thus, the first function is mainly characterized by transactional leadership qualities. The second function is best defined by high weights on items 12, 13, and 21, indicating that this function can be best described as a charismatic dimension.

The group centroids are plotted in Figure 1 (p. 24). Leaders of homogeneous groups were high on both the transactional leadership dimension,

Table 2. Standardized Canonical Weights

Discriminating items		Function 1: Transactional	Function 2: Charismatic
6.	"I do not change anything as long as things are going along all right."	.74	.34
9.	"I am impulsive about change."	1.31	−.07
†12.	"I would constantly create situations for others to learn."	1.64	−1.77
13.	"I would set people up in experiences where they learn."	−.54	1.44
18.	"I would be satisfied with performance as long as the old ways work."	−1.18	−.25
19.	"I exhibit confidence in others' ability to meet expectations."	.58	.06
21.	"I would tell people what to do if they want to be rewarded for their efforts."	.31	1.12
26.	"I would talk about special commendations and rewards for good work."	−1.59	−.04

scoring over one and a half deviations above the mean ($M = 1.53$), and on the charismatic dimension, scoring about a half deviation above the mean ($M = 0.40$). In contrast, leaders of high-heterogeneous groups were low on both dimensions, scoring about a half standard deviation below the mean on the transactional leadership dimension ($M = -0.32$), and scoring more than one deviation below the mean on the charismatic dimension ($M = -1.22$). Leaders

---

† Because item 12 presents high weights on both functions, we examined the values of the structure coefficients for this item as a further aid to the interpretation of the functions. While the standardized weights are raw weights multiplied by their respective standard deviation, the structure coefficients are the correlation between the functions and the original variables (Tatsuoka, 1988). The structure coefficients for item 12 were $C = -.07$ and $C = -.16$ for the first and second function, respectively. Thus, these results further suggest that item 12 contributes more significantly to function 2.

Figure 1. Group Centroids from Discriminant Analysis

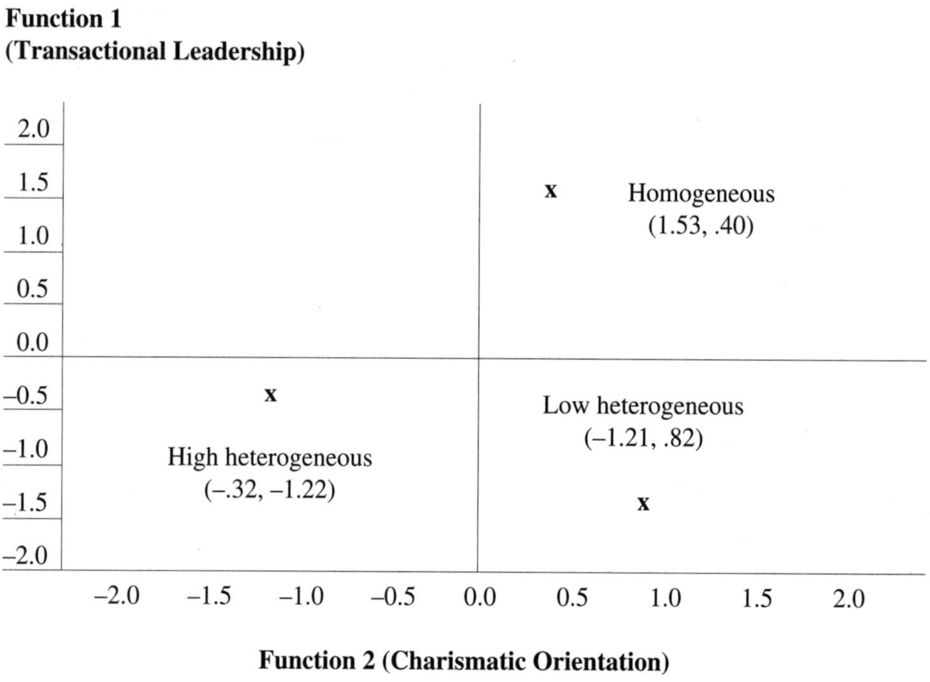

Function 1
(Transactional Leadership)

```
 2.0 |
     |
 1.5 |                               x        Homogeneous
     |                                        (1.53, .40)
 1.0 |
     |
 0.5 |
     |
 0.0 |
     |
-0.5 |              x                 Low heterogeneous
     |                                (-1.21, .82)
-1.0 |         High heterogeneous
     |           (-.32, -1.22)
-1.5 |                                      x
     |
-2.0 |
     |_____
        -2.0  -1.5  -1.0  -0.5  0.0  0.5  1.0  1.5  2.0
```

Function 2 (Charismatic Orientation)

of low-heterogeneous groups scored more than one standard deviation below the mean on the transactional dimension ($M = -1.21$), but almost one standard deviation above the mean on the charismatic dimension ($M = 0.82$).

Together, as presented in Table 3, these 2 functions correctly classified 83.3% of group leaders, including 80% of the leaders of homogeneous groups, 90% of the leaders of low-heterogeneous groups, and 80% of the leaders of high-heterogeneous groups. These probabilities represent an increment of approximately 50% over the prior probabilities. Thus, these results suggest that: (1) Measures of transactional leadership rather than charismatic leadership better discriminate between leaders of heterogeneous and homogeneous groups based on their self-evaluations, and (2) leaders of high-heterogeneous groups report displaying less transactional and charismatic behaviors than leaders of homogeneous groups.

Question 4. To test the idea that leaders of heterogeneous groups report lower ratings on leadership effectiveness than leaders of homogeneous groups, we conducted a bivariate correlation between gender heterogeneity and leaders' self-perceptions of effectiveness. Results indicate that diversity shows statistically significant negative correlations with leaders' self-

Table 3. Classification Results of Discriminant Analysis

		Predicted group membership					
		1		2		3	
Leaders' actual group	No. of cases	*M*	%	*M*	%	*M*	%
Homogeneous groups	10	8	80%	1	10%	1	10%
Low-heterogeneous groups	10	0	0%	9	90%	1	10%
High-heterogeneous groups	10	0	0%	2	20%	8	80%

M = Number of cases in each predicted group.

Note. Percentage of grouped cases correctly classified = 83.3%. Group 1 = leaders of homogeneous groups, Group 2 = leaders of low-heterogeneous groups, Group 3 = leaders of high-heterogeneous groups.

perceptions of effectiveness ($r = -.31$, $p < .05$), indicating that these decrease as the level of diversity increases in the group.

Question 5. To explore the question that leaders of heterogeneous groups experience more negative feelings than leaders of homogeneous groups, we computed a bivariate correlation between group heterogeneity and leaders' reports of feelings of happiness. Findings showed that there was a significant negative correlation between diversity and feelings of happiness ($r = -.46$, $p < .01$), indicating that leaders' feelings of happiness decrease as the level of diversity increases in the group.

Question 6. Correlation analysis conducted to assess the relationship between group diversity and leaders' reports of role ambiguity revealed a significant positive relationship ($r = .30$, $p < .05$). These findings suggest that, relative to leaders of homogeneous groups, leaders of heterogeneous groups find it more difficult to predict the behaviors of other group members and to identify appropriate standards of group behavior.

Question 7. To examine the idea that group heterogeneity is negatively related to leaders' use of hard-influence tactics and positively related to their use of soft-influence tactics, we computed bivariate correlations between gender heterogeneity and leaders' reports on hard- and soft-influence tactics respectively. The findings showed that leaders of heterogeneous groups reported using hard tactics of influence less frequently than leaders of homogeneous groups ($r = -.39, p < .01$). However, there was no evidence of differences in the use of soft tactics of influence between leaders of heterogeneous and homogeneous groups. In order to isolate the effects of diversity on influence tactics, we computed a partial correlation between gender heterogeneity and soft-influence tactics, controlling for role ambiguity, charismatic and transactional leadership, leader effectiveness, and hard tactics. The partial correlation showed that there was a positive significant relationship between group diversity and leaders' reports of using soft tactics ($r = .33, p < .05$), indicating that leaders of heterogeneous groups report using soft influence, such as seeking participation and arousing interest in the task, more frequently than leaders of homogeneous groups. The relationship between group heterogeneity and hard-influence tactics was unchanged after controlling for role ambiguity, charismatic and transactional leadership, leader effectiveness, and soft tactics ($r = -.41, p < .01$), indicating that leaders of heterogeneous groups report using hard tactics, such as persistent reminders, less frequently than leaders of homogeneous groups.

Discussion and Implications

This study contributes to the diversity literature by providing some evidence of the effects of group heterogeneity on leaders. Unlike previous studies on diversity, which have examined the effects of group diversity on group members (e.g., Jackson et al., 1991), this study has explored the effects of group diversity on leaders' perceptions of their work groups and themselves. Overall, the results of the present study suggest that leaders of heterogeneous groups perceive more negatively the work group and themselves. It seems that managing demographically diverse work groups takes a toll on leaders. In particular, compared to leaders of homogeneous groups, leaders of heterogeneous groups: (1) Describe the work group as less socially integrated and less stimulating, (2) view themselves with less transactional leadership qualities (e.g., less able to reward group members), (3) believe that they are less effective leaders, (4) report greater difficulty in predicting the reactions and behaviors of group members, (5) are more likely to experience feelings of sadness, and (6) report a lower use of hard tactics to influence group members (e.g., less likely to use persistent reminders) but a higher use of soft tactics (e.g., more likely to seek group members' participation).

These results are consistent with previous literature on diversity. Based on Byrne's (1971) similarity-attraction paradigm, studies have shown that heterogeneous groups are less socially integrated than homogeneous groups (O'Reilly et al., 1989). Our findings are consistent with this line of research by suggesting that leaders of heterogeneous groups also perceive group members as being less cohesive. Regarding the group climate, increased diversity is often associated with prejudice and stereotyping creating emotions of discomfort among group members (Jackson et al., 1995). Our findings are also consistent with this literature, supporting the notion that leaders of heterogeneous groups perceive the climate of their groups more negatively.

A possible explanation for these results relies on the similarity-attraction paradigm and the notion of leaders' self-blame. On the one hand, the similarity-attraction paradigm posits that individuals are more attracted to those similar to them (Berscheid, 1982; Byrne, 1971). Thus, diversity creates a context in which people are more likely to feel tension, anxiety, fear, frustration, and discomfort when interacting with other group members (Jackson et al., 1995). On the other hand, leaders are held responsible for group processes and outcomes (Hollander, 1978). Thus, it is possible that leaders would blame themselves for the challenges associated with diversity resulting in their negative view of the group and themselves.

It is interesting to compare the results of this study with the findings of the followers study (Mayo et al., 1994). Leaders and followers differ in the dominant dimension of leadership used to evaluate leaders and the degree to which they evaluate leadership attributes. Although "transactional" leadership becomes more prominent for leaders, "charismatic" leadership becomes more prominent for followers. Also, although leaders perceive themselves negatively, followers perceive their leaders positively. Bass and Avolio (1990) compared self and followers' ratings of transactional and transformational leadership. They found that leaders' perceptions are generally consistent with ratings generated by followers. Thus, it seems that the inconsistency between leaders' and followers' ratings may be related to the context of diversity in which leaders and followers interact.

A reasonable explanation for this leader-follower disagreement in the context of diversity may be that followers may consider a charismatic relationship with the leader a better way to cope with the emotional discomfort associated with diversity. Then this need for charisma may result in followers' exaggerated attributions of charisma to their leaders. In contrast, leaders may focus more on conventional ways of leadership (e.g., transactional and exchange) because they prefer to rely on well-known patterns of behavior to avoid uncertainty and emotional involvement. Additionally, leaders may have a negative view of themselves rather than a positive one, as attributed to them by their followers. As already mentioned, this negative self-image as leader may be the result of self-blame for the challenges encountered in the group.

Although this is an exploratory study and additional research is clearly necessary, these results offer some practical implications for managing diversity in the workplace. Because of the negative effects of diversity on leaders' perceptions of their groups and themselves, diversity training that makes supervisors aware of these challenges would be useful. Also, since members of heterogeneous groups seem to prefer charismatic leadership (Mayo et al., 1994), supervisors may benefit from training courses that emphasize charismatic behaviors, such as giving a mission to the group and establishing emotional relationships with employees. Finally, recruitment practices that consider charismatic behaviors as criteria for selection of potential leaders of heterogeneous groups may also help to effectively manage diversity in the workplace.

A number of extensions of this line of research are possible and desirable. First, a field study examining the relationship between diversity and leadership would complement the present study. In our study, group members had a limited time frame for interaction, and gender was the only demographic attribute used to define the relative composition of the group. In organizations, group members would have prolonged and continuous exposure to each other and to the leader, and several demographic attributes such as gender, race, age, tenure, and education can also be explored. Second, issues of membership stability could not be addressed within this experimental design. However, it would be valuable to examine the relationship between diversity, leadership, and turnover. It is possible that leaders of heterogeneous groups experience higher turnover rates than leaders of homogeneous groups. Managing diversity efforts may benefit from this line of research, which will contribute to the understanding of diversity and its implications for leadership practices.

References

Bass, B. M. (1985). *Leadership and performance beyond expectations.* New York: Free Press.

Bass, B. M. (1990). *Bass & Stogdill's handbook of leadership* (3rd ed.). New York: Free Press.

Bass, B. M., & Avolio, B. J. (1990). *Manual: The Multifactor Leadership Questionnaire.* Palo Alto, CA: Consulting Psychologists Press.

Bem, D. J. (1972). Self-perception theory. In L. Berkowitz (Ed.), *Advances in experimental social psychology* (Vol. 6, pp. 1-62). New York: Academic Press.

Berscheid, E. (1982). Attraction and emotion in interpersonal relationships. In M. S. Clark & S. T. Fiske (Eds.), *Affect and cognition: The 17th annual Carnegie Symposium on cognition* (pp. 37-54). Hillsdale, NJ: Erlbaum.

Burns, J. M. (1978). *Leadership.* New York: Harper & Row.

Byrne, D. E. (1971). *The attraction paradigm.* New York: Academic Press.

Cartwright, D. (1968). The nature of group cohesiveness. In D. Cartwright & A. Zander (Eds.), *Group dynamics: Research and theory* (3rd ed., pp. 91-109). New York: Harper & Row.

Conger, J. A. (1989). *The charismatic leaders: Beyond the mystique of exceptional leadership.* San Francisco: Jossey-Bass.

Conger, J. A., & Kanungo, R. N. (1988). *Charismatic leadership: The elusive factor in organizational effectiveness.* San Francisco: Jossey-Bass.

Dean, J. W., & Bowen, D. A. (1994). Management theory and total quality: Improving research and practice through theory development. *Academy of Management Review, 19*(3), 392-418.

Devine, P. G., Monteith, M. J., Zuwerink, J. R., & Elliot, A. J. (1991). Prejudice with and without compunction. *Journal of Personality and Social Psychology, 60,* 817-830.

Falbe, C. M., & Yukl, G. (1992). Consequences for managers of using single influence tactics and combination of tactics. *Academy of Management Journal, 35*(3), 638-652.

Farris, G. F., & Lim, P. G. (1969). Effects of performance on leadership, cohesiveness, influence, satisfaction, and subsequent performance. *Journal of Applied Psychology, 53,* 490-497.

Forsyth, D. R. (1990). *Group dynamics.* Pacific Grove, CA: Brooks/Cole.

French, J. R., & Raven, B. (1959). The bases of social power. In D. Cartwright (Ed.), *Studies in social power.* Ann Arbor: University of Michigan, Institute for Social Research.

Goodstadt, B. E., & Kipnis, D. (1970). Situational influences on the use of power. *Journal of Applied Psychology, 54,* 201-207.

Graves, L. M., & Powell, G. N. (1994). *Effect of sex similarity on recruiters' evaluations of job applicants: Is communication a mediator?* Presented at the annual meeting of the Academy of Management, Dallas.

Hemphill, J. K. (1950). Relations between the size of the group and the behavior of "superior" leaders. *Journal of Social Psychology, 32,* 11-22.

Hollander, E. P. (1978). *Leadership dynamics: A practical guide to effective relationships.* New York: Free Press.

Ivancevich, J. M., & Matteson, M. T. (1980). *Stress and work: A managerial perspective.* Glenview, IL: Scott, Foresman.

Jackson, S. E. (1991). Team composition in organizational settings: Issues in managing an increasingly diverse workforce. In S. Worchel, W. Wood, & J. Simpson (Eds.), *Group process and productivity* (pp. 138-173). Beverly Hills: Sage.

Jackson, S. E., & Alvarez, E. B. (1992). Working through diversity as a strategic impera-
tive. In S. E. Jackson (Ed.), *Diversity in the workplace: Human resources initiatives*
(pp. 13-29). New York: Guilford Press.

Jackson, S. E., Brett, J. F., Sessa, V. I., Cooper, D. M., Julin, J. A., & Peyronnin, K.
(1991). Some differences make a difference: Individual dissimilarity and group
heterogeneity as correlates of recruitment, promotions, and turnover. *Journal of
Applied Psychology, 76,* 675-689.

Jackson, S. E., May, K. E., & Whitney, K. (1995). Understanding the dynamics of
diversity in decision making teams. In R. A. Guzzo & E. Salas (Eds.), *Team decision
making effectiveness in organizations.* San Francisco: Jossey-Bass.

James, L. R., & Jones, A. P. (1974). Organizational climate: A review of theory and
research. *Psychological Bulletin, 81,* 1096-1112.

Klecka, W. R. (1980). *Discriminant analysis.* Beverly Hills: Sage.

Kotter, J. P. (1985). *Power and influence.* New York: Free Press.

Lincoln, J. R., & Miller, J. (1979). Work and friendship ties in organizations: A comparative analysis of relational networks. *Administrative Science Quarterly, 24,* 181-199.

Lott, A. J., & Lott, B. E. (1965). Group cohesiveness and interpersonal attraction: A
review of relationships with antecedent and consequent variables. *Psychological
Bulletin, 4,* 259-302.

Mayo, M. C., Meindl, J. R., & Pastor, J.-C. (1994). *Diversity and leadership: The effects
of group diversity on the emergence of charismatic leadership.* Presented at the annual
meeting of the Academy of Management, Dallas.

McCain, B. E., O'Reilly, C. A., III, & Pfeffer, J. (1983). The effects of departmental
demography on turnover: The case of a university. *Academy of Management Journal,
26,* 626-641.

Meindl, J. R. (1990). On leadership: An alternative to the conventional wisdom. *Research
in Organizational Behavior, 22,* 159-203.

Morrison, A. M. (1992). *The new leaders: Guidelines on leadership diversity in America.*
San Francisco: Jossey-Bass.

O'Reilly, C. A., III, Caldwell, D. F., & Barnett, W. P. (1989). Work group, social
integration, and turnover. *Administrative Science Quarterly, 34,* 21-37.

Pfeffer, J., & O'Reilly, C. A., III (1987). Hospital demography and turnover among
nurses. *Industrial Relations, 26,* 158-173.

Rosenbaum, M. (1986). The repulsion hypothesis: On the nondevelopment of relationships. *Journal of Personality and Social Psychology, 51,* 1156-1166.

Ryle, G. (1949). *The concept of mind.* London: Hutchinson.

Shamir, B. (1992). Attribution of influence and charisma to the leader: The romance of
leadership revisited. *Journal of Applied Social Psychology, 22,* 386-407.

Tatsuoka, M. M. (1988). *Multivariate analysis: Techniques for educational and psychological research* (2nd ed.). New York: Macmillan.

Tsui, A. S., Egan, T. D., & O'Reilly, C. A., III (1992). Being different: Relational
demography and organizational attachment. *Administrative Science Quarterly, 37,* 549-
579.

Wagner, W. G., Pfeffer, J., & O'Reilly, C. A., III (1984). Organizational demography and
turnover in top management groups. *Administrative Science Quarterly, 29,* 74-92.

Walton, R. W., & Hackman, J. R. (1986). Groups under contrasting management strategies. In P. S. Goodman (Ed.), *Designing effective work groups.* San Francisco: Jossey-Bass.

Yukl, G. (1994). *Leadership in organizations.* Englewood, NJ: Prentice Hall.

Yukl, G., & Falbe, C. M. (1990). Influence tactics and objectives in upward, downward, and lateral influence attempts. *Journal of Applied Psychology, 75*(2), 132-140.

Yukl, G., Falbe, C. M., & Joo, Y. Y. (1993). Patterns of influence behavior for managers. *Group and Organization Management, 18,* 5-28.

Yukl, G., & Tracey, B. J. (1992). Consequences of influence tactics used with subordinates, peers, and the boss. *Journal of Applied Psychology, 77*(4), 525-535.

CULTURE AND LEADERSHIP AMONG TAIWANESE AND U.S. WORKERS: DO VALUES INFLUENCE LEADERSHIP IDEALS?

Keith James
Dz-Lyang Chen
Russell Cropanzano

Department of Psychology
Colorado State University

Abstract

In this study, differences in general cultural values and leadership/ motivational ideals were compared between U.S. (N=80) and Taiwanese (N=102) samples. Differences in the relationships among values and ideals for the two groups were also examined. Both groups completed questionnaires, which supplied data for the study. U.S. workers were found to be less Collectivistic, lower in Uncertainty Avoidance, more Feminine, and less Paternalistic than the Taiwanese on cultural value dimensions. On leadership/motivational ideals, Americans endorsed Role Clarification, Contingent Reward, Contingent Punishment, and Reward Power more, and Expert Power less, than did the Taiwanese. In addition, several correlation patterns between values and ideals differed between the two samples. The limitations of the study and the need for further research and theory linking values, leadership and motivational ideals, and other work outcomes are discussed.

✳ ✳ ✳

Both foreign investment *by* the U.S. and foreign investment *in* the U.S. have increased steadily in recent years. American investment in developing countries has, in fact, increased at a faster rate than investment in developed countries (Ronen, 1986). These trends increasingly require managers to deal with people from different national and cultural backgrounds. As more and more companies become global, understanding the cultures of foreign-national employees and trading partners is becoming a factor critical to organizational effectiveness.

For instance, Cox (1991) argued that effective multicultural organizations must insure that core organizational goals, norms, practices, systems, and values are congruent with the various cultural perspectives held by different groups of employees. Success at doing this requires using cross-cultural research to study how the cultures of different groups interact with specific types of organizational features. In multinational corporations (MNCs), this means examining how the cultural values of the different nationality groups of workers within the companies might moderate the relationship between organizational practices and organizational success.

Hofstede (1980) identified four major cultural value dimensions and argued that they are crucial to the regulation of social systems and individual behavior. In particular, he described how they are important to organizational success by way of their effect on social relations and individual motivation. A variety of research (for example, see reviews and discussions in Dorfman & Howell, 1988; James, 1993a; Smith & Bond, 1993; and Triandis, 1989a) has substantiated both the existence of the dimensions Hofstede identified and their impact on a variety of individual and organizational outcomes.

Taiwan has become a major international economic power. It is also one of the main trading partners of the U.S. (U.S. Department of Commerce, 1992, cited in Wright, 1994). Not only do U.S. companies have a strong presence in Taiwan, but Taiwanese MNCs have also established an important presence in the U.S. (Kotkin, 1993).

The mainstream U.S. culture and the mainstream Taiwanese culture[†] may be very different on Hofstede's value dimensions (Hofstede, 1980). This may be important for the increasing numbers of Taiwanese and Americans who work together, but it has not been the subject of much research. It was the focus here, however. In particular, we examined how differences in cultural values between the two nations might have an impact on the effectiveness of leadership and motivational strategies in the workplace.

Culture: Definition and Dimensions

Hofstede (1980) defines culture as the collective mental programming of the people in an environment. This perspective emphasizes the "immutabil-

---

[†]Some evidence indicates that many U.S. ethnic minorities differ from the majority on some of Hofstede's cultural values, such as Individualism/Collectivism. Taiwan has its own minority groups and, though there is little research on their cultural values, these may also differ from those of the Taiwanese majority. Thus our emphasis here is on the use of members of the mainstream national cultures.

ity of mental programming" conditioned by common environments and beliefs among a large group of people (p. 43; see also Triandis, 1972). Although we may all be conditioned by cultural influences at many different levels such as family, social group, and geographical region, Hofstede claimed that national culture has the greatest impact on organizational behavior.

Cross-cultural researchers tend to describe culture in terms of value dimensions. A value is an enduring belief that a specific mode of conduct or end-state of existence is personally or socially preferable to an opposite or converse mode of conduct or end-state of existence (Rokeach, 1973). That is, values are global beliefs about desirable end-states not tied to any specific object or situation. Values seem capable of broad influences on emotions, thinking, and behavior (Hofstede, 1980; Rokeach, 1973; Triandis, 1989b). They are also standards that guide and determine action, attitudes toward objects and situations, and ideology. In contrast, an attitude is an orientation toward a specific object and situation. It results from the application of a general value to concrete objects or situations (Davis & Rasool, 1988). Behavior is viewed as the overt manifestation of attitudes and values. Thus, the role of values, in the cultural influence model, is: culture—> values—> attitudes—> intention—> behavior.

Perhaps the most frequently cited, discussed, and replicated cultural value dimensions are those derived from Hofstede's (1980) empirical research. He conducted a large-scale cross-cultural study that examined values among individuals from 53 independent nations. Four factors were derived that seemed to distinguish among the cultures of these countries: Power Distance indicates the extent to which a society accepts the fact that power and other rewards in institutions and organizations are distributed unequally. In other words, it assesses the extent to which hierarchical social relations and disparities in power are generally endorsed. Uncertainty Avoidance indicates the extent to which individuals feel threatened by uncertain and ambiguous situations and the extent they try to avoid them. It reflects the need for security and the establishment of many formal rules to reduce anxiety triggered by a lack of clarity about expected or acceptable behavior. Individualism/ Collectivism is usually treated as a bipolar dimension. Individualism implies a loosely knit social framework in which people are supposed to take care only of themselves and their immediate families. On the other hand, Collectivism is characterized by a tight social framework in which people distinguish strongly between (larger than family-unit) in-groups and out-groups and show care and concern for all in-group members. Masculinity expresses the extent to which the dominant values in society are those typical of the "masculine" sex role. That is, assertiveness, focus on acquisition of money and objects, and limited emotional involvement with others are emphasized. Hofstede (1980; see also Triandis, 1989a) presents evidence that these four values are central to the nature of both societal and individual-psychological functioning.

Paternalism is another value dimension that has recently been added to Hofstede's four cultural dimensions, based on studies of management practices in some Asian countries. Paternalism generally indicates that managers take a personal interest in workers' off-the-job lives and personal problems and attempt to promote workers' personal welfare and help them achieve personal goals. For instance, Uhl-Bien, Tierney, Graen, and Wakabayashi (1990) found that Japanese line managers' degree of belief that their supervisors were strong on paternalism positively influenced their working relationships with their supervisors, their overall job satisfaction, and both their formal and informal career investment.

Hofstede's four dimensions and Paternalism seem to be very basic cultural values that influence a number of important outcomes. The descriptive and predictive utility of these factors have been replicated independently more than once (e.g., Hofstede & Bond, 1984; Ng, Hossain, Ball, Bond, Hayashi, Lim, O'Driscoll, Sinha, & Yang, 1982), and they have proven to be relevant to a number of personal (e.g., Gudykunst & Ting-Toomey, 1988; James, 1993b; Triandis, 1989b) and organizational (e.g., Dorfman & Howell, 1988; Hofstede, 1980; James, 1993a; Ng et al., 1982) outcomes.

Cultural Values of Taiwan and Mainstream U.S. Cultures

Mainstream U.S. culture and the culture of Taiwan belong to different cultural clusters, according to Hofstede (1980). Taiwan is a country whose main population emigrated recently from south China, bringing with it traditional Chinese culture. In Hofstede's seminal work, *Culture's Consequences* (1980), Taiwan's national values were described as relatively high in Collectivism and Power Distance, relatively strong on Uncertainty Avoidance, and relatively Feminine. In contrast, the mainstream U.S. culture was characterized as having relatively high Individualism, relatively low Power Distance, relatively low Uncertainty Avoidance, and relatively high Masculinity.

Other data make these patterns appear less clear-cut, however. Although Chinese culture is the main component of Taiwanese culture, Japanese rule before World War II and the influence of American culture after the war have made Taiwanese culture unique. Meindl, Hunt, and Lee (1989), in fact, found Taiwan closer to the mainstream culture of the U.S. than to mainland China on the Individualism/Collectivism dimension. Chen (1988) also found that Taiwanese are significantly more individualistic than mainland Chinese. In addition, Taiwan may not, in fact, be a feminine culture. Dorfman and Howell (1988) found that their Taiwanese subjects were actually more masculine than their American sample. Finally, Chang (1985) provided evidence indicating that Taiwanese culture also promotes high valuation of paternalism relative to mainstream U.S. culture. He found, in a survey from American and Taiwanese managers in a U.S. company in Taiwan, that the Taiwanese, but not the Americans, endorsed paternalistic values as very important. These ideas lead to our first hypothesis:

> *Hypothesis 1:* There will be differences between U.S. and Taiwanese individuals on the four Hofstede values and on Paternalism. Specifically, compared with Taiwanese, Americans will exhibit higher Individualism, lower Power Distance, lower Masculinity, weaker Uncertainty Avoidance, and less of a Paternalistic orientation.

Cultural Values and Leadership and Motivational Ideals

The value differences outlined above may create important differences in the expectations of Taiwanese and Americans about organizational policies and practices, but this possibility has not been the subject of much research. Leadership (e.g., control and coordination of workers) and motivation (e.g., activation of workers' energies in service of organizational ends) are crucial to organizational success and survival (Kanfer, 1990; Yukl, 1989). If cultural values lead employees from different cultures to have different ways of organizing behavior and different implicit leadership theories, then organizations may need to employ somewhat different strategies for different groups in order to be effective. Thus, we explored potential differences between U.S. and Taiwanese workers in how cultural values seem to relate to leadership ideals and the effectiveness of different motivational strategies.

Leadership has been one of the most studied organizational issues. Unfortunately, there has been little direct research on how cultural values influence leadership activities and their effectiveness (Bhagat, Kedia, Crawford, & Kaplan, 1990). Rodrigues (1990), however, has described possible relationships among Hofstede's four dimensions and House and Mitchell's (1974) four (situation-linked) leadership styles—directive, supportive, achievement (charisma), and participative.

According to Rodrigues' (1990) theory, a directive leadership style (i.e., specification of assignments, specification of procedures to use, high use of legitimate and coercive influence) will be more effective in those societies, such as Taiwan, with relatively high power distance, collectivism, and uncertainty avoidance. A supportive style (e.g., direct supervisory support, role clarification) is suitable for societies with moderate power distance and collectivism. Moreover, an achievement style (contingent reward, contingent punishment, charisma [leader achievement], and use of expert power) can work well in those societies, such as the mainstream U.S. culture, with weak-to-moderate uncertainty avoidance. Finally, a participative style (participation in decisions, leader representation of subordinates in the organization, use of referent-power influence) can work well everywhere except in those societies with a combination of relatively high power distance, strong collectivism, and high uncertainty avoidance, which should make it ineffective in Taiwan.

Hofstede (1980) presented an alternative possibility. He argues that in cultures relatively high in uncertainty avoidance and power distance (such as Taiwan), behavior of individual leaders will be relatively unimportant. Instead, organization-level norms, policies, and structures will be largely responsible for shaping individual motivation, performance, and other aspects of work behavior. Both Rodrigues' and Hofstede's conceptions about leadership and motivation have gone largely untested, however.

In the present study, Taiwanese and U.S. workers' perceptions of nine potential leader actions were examined, which reflected House's four styles of leadership (House & Mitchell, 1974) that Rodrigues (1990) incorporated into his cultural-leadership model. The nine leader actions were: role clarification, work assignment, specification of procedures, supportiveness, contingent reward, contingent punishment, achievement (charisma), participation, and representation. According to Podsakoff, Dorfman, Howell, and Todor (1986) and Podsakoff and Schriesheim (1985), these dimensions are more central to successfully guiding and motivating employees than the commonly studied "task" or "interpersonal skill" leadership dimensions. In addition, we examined cultural influences on reactions to French and Raven's (1959) five categories of leader influence strategies—coercive power, expert power, legitimate power, referent power, and reward power.

Based on the ideas and information of Rodrigues (1990) and Hofstede (1980) outlined above, we generated two possibilities for differences between Taiwanese and U.S. nationals in endorsement of these leadership strategies:

Hypothesis 2a (based on Rodrigues, 1990): There will be differences between Americans and Taiwanese in ideals for leadership and motivation. Specifically, U.S. workers will endorse the components of supportive, achievement (charisma), and participative leadership styles more than the Taiwanese, who will endorse the components of directive leadership more than the U.S. workers.

Hypothesis 2b (based on Hofstede, 1980): All leadership and motivational strategies will be viewed as less important by Taiwanese than by U.S. workers and, thus, endorsed more weakly.

Relations of Values to Leadership and Motivational Ideals

While Hofstede examined values at the national (i.e., aggregate) level, we assessed them at the individual level. That is, values can be looked upon as either characteristics of cultures or characteristics of individuals (Triandis, 1989a). The two levels are related, however, because individuals are more likely to be inclined toward the dominant values of their culture (Triandis, 1989a; Wallace, 1971). Thus, a pattern exists in which individuals within a culture exhibit probabilistic patterns of value consistency internally and mean difference relative to other cultures, while at the same time having some internal variability (Wallace, 1971). Moreover, variations in value scores among individuals within one culture are likely to have different relations to behavioral intentions and behaviors than the variations among individuals in another culture on the same value because each value comes into play relative to the social and physical environments, social norms, and entire cultural system of each particular culture (see also Hsu, 1971; Triandis, 1989a). For these reasons, we expected the range of scores on particular values to show differential patterns of relation to specific leadership ideals and motivational strategies for the Taiwanese sample versus the U.S. one.

Differences in reactions to contingent reward and contingent punishment have been found in comparisons among Americans, Mexicans, and Taiwanese (Dorfman & Howell, 1988; Podsakoff et al., 1986). And, as was noted above, Chang (1985) found that Taiwanese managers endorsed paternalistic actions much more than did American managers. Direct, systematic tests of the relationships between the values of Taiwanese and U.S. workers and their reactions to leadership and motivational strategies are lacking, however.

Based on the differences in the cultural systems in Taiwan and the U.S. that we outlined earlier based on the research of Chang (1985), Chen (1988),

Dorfman and Howell (1988), Hofstede (1980), Meindl et al. (1989), and Podsakoff et al. (1986), we generated the following hypothesis:

> *Hypothesis 3*: Different values-to-leadership-ideals patterns will exist for Taiwanese and U.S. subjects. Specifically, Paternalism, Individualism/Collectivism, Power Distance, and Uncertainty Avoidance are expected to correlate positively with endorsement of directive actions and negatively with endorsement of participation among Taiwanese. Paternalism is not expected to be related to leadership ideals among U.S. workers. Masculinity/Femininity, Individualism/Collectivism, and Uncertainty Avoidance should correlate negatively with endorsement of supportive and participative leadership actions for U.S. workers.

Method

Subjects

Participants included 102 Taiwanese (68 men and 34 women) and 80 U.S. (44 men and 36 women) workers. Taiwanese participants were all full-time employees from one of 8, mostly high-tech, companies. Their average age was 30.4; 29% had advanced degrees; and 34 of them were either currently supervisors or had supervisory experiences. The U.S. participants were mainly of European descent, and were all full-time employees from one of 10, mostly high-tech, companies. Eighteen were supervisors and 62 were subordinates. Their average age was 32.7; 34% had advanced degrees. In both samples, participants held a variety of jobs, with engineers being the largest single group. There was no significant difference between the samples in average education level. Although there was a significant difference in mean age (30.4 versus 32.7), it was small, and the age range was similar with the largest percentage of subjects for both countries being between 26 and 35. The U.S. sample was essentially half male and half female, and the Taiwanese sample was only one-third female. The sex ratio here roughly reflected the overall labor-market gender composition in each country. Because the difference in the sex compositions of the samples might have affected scores on the variables of interest, sex of subjects was included in the data analyses.

Measures

A questionnaire completed by the subjects contained scales for the five values, the leadership actions, and the influence strategies. Each scale is described below.

Work values. A 32-item value scale, developed by Dorfman and Howell (1988) to measure Hofstede's (1980) 4 cultural value dimensions (Individualism/Collectivism, Power Distance, Uncertainty Avoidance, and Femininity/Masculinity) plus Paternalism, was used in this study. This instrument has been tested in cross-cultural contexts and has proved to have satisfactory reliability and apparent validity (see Dorfman & Howell, 1988). The respondents indicated their opinions about each value item on a 5-point scale from "strongly disagree" to "strongly agree."

Leadership/motivation ideals. In the current research, 9 scales developed and validated by different authors (see below) were used to assess individuals' reactions to several potential leader behaviors linked to House's Path-goal leadership theory (see House & Mitchell, 1974). The 9 scales were: Role Clarification, Work Assignment, Specification of Procedures, and Supportiveness (from Schriesheim, 1978); Contingent Reward and Contingent Punishment (from Podsakoff et al., 1986); and Achievement (Charisma), Participation, and Representation (from Dorfman, Howell, Cotton, & Tate, 1992). For the current research, respondents were asked to respond to these items relative to their beliefs about how an *ideal leader* should behave, regardless of what their current supervisor actually did.

In addition, a 20-item instrument developed by Hinkin and Schriesheim (1989) was used to measure perceptions of French and Raven's (1959) 5 power bases (legitimate, referent, reward, coercive, and expert power). Hinkin and Schriesheim (1989) presented evidence for the internal consistency reliability, clean-factor structure, content validity, discriminant validity, and criterion-related validity of this instrument.

Scale Translation

The Taiwanese participants filled out a Chinese-language version of the research questionnaires. The Chinese versions of Hofstede's value dimensions and the leadership behavior scales were developed by Dorfman and Howell (1988), using translation and back translation. The influence-tactic questionnaire was translated into Chinese for this study by a Taiwanese linguist who had long experience working in Taiwan. Another bilingual scientist then did a back translation, and we checked the equivalence of the two versions. In addition, the newly translated Chinese version was pretested with native Taiwanese to assure the clarity of item wordings.

Results

We first examined the reliability (internal consistency) of each of the inventories we employed. Then we used MANOVAs to compare value, leader behavior, and influence strategy scores between the U.S. and Taiwanese subsamples. Finally, we tested for differential relationships between values and ideal leader behaviors and strategies by correlating each value with each behavior and strategy separately for each subsample and using z-tests to compare correlations between the samples.

Reliabilities

A few scales had fairly low internal-consistency reliabilities for one or the other national group (e.g., .47 for the specifying procedures leader behavior in the U.S. sample; it was .79 among Taiwanese). Generally, however, the reliabilities were reasonably good, ranging from .60 (contingent-punishment leader behavior) to .88 (contingent-reward leader behavior).

MANOVAs on Values and Ideals

MANOVAs yielded significant ($p < .05$) multivariate-Fs for the main effect of nationality on values, ideal leader behaviors, and leader influence strategies. Results from these analyses are shown in Table 1. Gender also had significant main effects on cultural values and preferred influence strategies. Means, standard deviations, and univariate Fs for these effects are shown in Table 2. None of the interactions of gender and nationality were significant.

Hypothesis 1 predicted that there would be differences between the work values of Taiwanese and Americans. This was generally supported. All expected significant differences on values were obtained except for that of Power Distance. The differences between the two samples for Collectivism were, however, not as high as previously reported (see also Dorfman & Howell, 1988; Hofstede, 1980). The Collectivism scores of U.S. workers were somewhat higher than in previous studies, while those of Taiwanese workers were somewhat lower than expected. The explanation for this might be that, unlike the pattern in some countries such as Japan, collectivism in Taiwan seems more important relative to family than within work settings (Hsu, 1971). On the other hand, the U.S. sample was from high-technology

Table 1. Univariate Values for Variables with Significant Nationality MANOVA Results

Variables	U.S. Mean	*SD*	Taiwan Mean	*SD*	*F*
Hofstede Cultural Value Dimensions					
Collectivism	3.08	0.67	3.46	0.61	7.52**
Uncertainty Avoidance	4.00	0.48	4.17	0.42	4.17*
Masculinity	1.87	0.71	2.93	0.62	105.97***
Paternalism	2.42	0.70	3.42	0.52	86.54***
Leadership Behaviors					
Support	5.83	0.67	5.49	0.96	4.04*
Role Clarification	6.14	0.82	5.31	0.92	27.38***
Work Assignment	5.00	0.99	5.32	1.03	4.67*
Contingent Reward	6.05	0.71	5.46	1.14	10.32**
Contingent Punishment	5.54	0.92	5.00	0.83	12.91***
Leadership Influence Strategies					
Reward Power	3.49	0.60	2.93	0.64	25.37**
Coercive Power	1.55	0.44	1.76	0.53	4.95*
Expert Power	4.06	0.55	4.32	0.45	11.77***

Note: U.S. *N* is 80 for the Cultural Value measures and 62 for the Leadership Behaviors and Leadership Influence Strategies. Taiwanese *N* is 102 for Cultural Values and 101 for Leadership Behaviors and Influence Strategies.

***$p \leq .001$, **$p \leq .01$, *$p \leq .05$

Table 2. Means and Univariate *F*s for Variables Showing Significant Sex Effects

	Female	Male	Univariate *F* Values
Hofstede Cultural Value Dimensions			
Collectivism	3.13	3.39	8.07*
Masculinity	2.06	2.71	33.93**
Leadership Influence Strategies			
Expert Power	4.32	4.17	5.92*

Note: Female *N* is 70 for the two Cultural Value scores and 66 for Expert Power. Male *N* is 112 for the Cultural Value scores and 99 for Expert Power.

**$p \leq .01$, *$p \leq .05$

companies, which tend to encourage teamwork. This may have contributed to higher than normal Collectivism scores in the U.S. sample.

The largest between-country difference on values found in this study was in Masculinity, with the Taiwanese subjects having the higher Masculinity scores. This contradicts Hofstede's (1980) findings but replicates those of Dorfman and Howell (1988). Males had, as would be expected, higher scores on Masculinity than did females, and the Taiwanese sample had a higher proportion of men than did the U.S. one. Yet gender effects were controlled for by including gender in the analysis, and the main effect of nationality on Masculinity/Femininity scores was still significant. This fits with the fact that Taiwanese culture has more negative stereotypes of women and greater male-female status differentials than does mainstream U.S. culture.

Hypothesis 2a predicted differences between the two national samples on ideal leadership actions or behaviors and influence strategy preferences. These predictions were also supported to some extent. The leadership-behavior scales, which showed significant differences, had Americans more than the Taiwanese describing their ideal leaders as behaving Supportively, engaging in Role Clarification, and administering Contingent Rewards and Punishments. The Taiwanese subjects, though, endorsed Clarifying of Work Assignments by leaders more. The results are congruent with the characteristics of Taiwanese versus U.S. business practices. Taiwanese employees are used to ambiguous roles because job rotations and multiple role assignments for individuals are quite common. But this means that they have a great need for supervisors to specify tasks and task priorities. American companies, on the other hand, tend to have clearer role distinctions and typically employ fairly detailed job descriptions. Taiwanese organizations also tend to be flatter than those in the U.S.—that is, to have fewer levels of hierarchy. The relatively hierarchic nature of American companies and the clearer distinction between administrative and other roles should encourage use of contingent reward and punishment (see, e.g., Beauvois & Dubois, 1988).

Congruent with the contingent-reward result just described, our American workers endorsed Reward Power as an influence strategy more than the Taiwanese employees. In contrast, Taiwanese endorsed Expert Power and Coercive Power more than Americans.

The prediction in *Hypothesis 2b,* that Taiwanese would generally view leader behavior as less important, also received a bit of support. The significant multivariate-F for the leader-behavior variables (see Table 1) indicates that Taiwanese subjects generally (i.e., summed across all leader-behavior types) gave lower ratings on this group of variables. Thus, as Hofstede (1980) argued, in addition to different unique patterns for specific leader ideals between the two cultures, individual leader behavior may be *generally* somewhat less important to Taiwanese than to U.S. workers. Finally, females preferred Expert Power as an influence tactic more than males.

The Relationship between Values and Ideals

Hypothesis 3 stated that values would be differentially related to the two national samples' leadership ideals. To test this, the significance of the difference in values/work-preference correlations between the U.S. and Taiwanese samples were examined. Correlations that were significant for one or more samples and significant *z*-scores for differences between the correlations for the two samples are shown in Table 3.

This hypothesis received mixed support. First, Collectivism was significantly more related to endorsement of leader's Specification of Procedures for the Taiwanese participants than for the U.S. sample. This makes some sense. Those high in individualism should, by definition, expect to act relatively independently. Collectivistic persons, at least in a collectivistic society, may expect more coordinated action. On the other hand, Collectivism was significantly more related to endorsement of Expert Power for Americans than for Taiwanese.

Somewhat unexpectedly, Uncertainty Avoidance was positively correlated with Role Clarification, Work Assignment, Specification of Procedure, Contingent Reward, and Contingent Punishment in *both* countries in this study. It correlated significantly more with Contingent Reward for Americans, however. American workers may find rewards more useful in providing feedback about the appropriateness of behavior; or they may feel more strongly that appropriate behavior deserves reward. The accuracy of these alternative explanations for this result should be examined in future research.

As expected, Power Distance was *positively* related to extent of endorsement of Legitimate Power for Taiwanese. Unexpectedly, Power Distance and endorsement of Legitimate Power were *negatively* related among Americans. The *z*-test for difference in these correlations was significant. Power-distance value scores were significantly associated with endorsement of Coercive Power among Taiwanese but not Americans. Power Distance also correlated negatively with endorsement of Participation as a leadership strategy in both samples, though significantly more so among Americans. Even though there was some variation between Taiwanese and U.S. workers, these results generally seem to fit with the meaning of the power-distance construct: Those who have high levels of this value are purported to generally

Table 3. Zero-order Correlations of Cultural Value Dimensions and Leadership Behaviors, and *z*-scores for Intersample Comparisons of Correlations

Scale	U.S. ($N = 62$)	Taiwan ($N = 101$)	z-score[a]
COL with Specification	.06	.34**	−1.70*
COL with Expert Power	.23*	−.10	2.00*
PD with Participation	−.55**	−.29**	−1.58*
PD with Legitimate Power	−.26*	.12	−2.30**
PD with Coercive Power	.07	.28**	
UA with Role Clarification	.22	.27**	
UA with Work Assignment	.30*	.28**	
UA with Specification	.24	.34**	
UA with Contingent Reward	.51**	.24*	1.64*
UA with Contingent Punish	.31*	.31*	
UA with Charisma	.34**	.18	
UA with Reward Power	.28*	.10	
UA with Expert Power	.31*	.28**	
MAS with Work Assignment	.29*	−.09	2.30**
MAS with Contingent Punish	−.28*	−.03	−1.52*
MAS with Participation	−.30*	−.18	
PAT with Support	.33**	.15	
PAT with Specification	.07	.35**	−1.70*
PAT with Contingent Punish	−.28*	−.02	−1.58*

Note: Only those cases where at least one correlation coefficient and/or the *z*-score reached .05 significance are reported. The probability of 8 of 18 correlations differing significantly between the two samples by chance is less than .01.

[a]*z*-score indicates the difference between two correlations.
*$p < .05$, **$p < .01$

Key:
COL	Collectivism
PD	Power Distance
UA	Uncertainty Avoidance
MAS	Masculinity
PAT	Paternalism

feel that possession of any high-status social position gives the incumbent widespread power and authority. The somewhat lower negative correlation of Power Distance and endorsement of participative leadership among Taiwanese may reflect influences of Japanese culture and organizations (of which there are many in Taiwan), which promote some participative practices (e.g., the Ringi decision-making system, in which proposals are systematically passed up and down the organizational hierarchy) despite relatively high levels of Power Distance. Power Distance scores were also significantly associated with endorsement of Coercive Power among Taiwanese but not among Americans. This may reflect a sense in Taiwan that high-status individuals have a wide latitude in judging others, and low-status individuals have little right to expect good treatment (see, e.g., Gudykunst & Ting-Toomey, 1988); while in the U.S., status, as well as its associated rights and privileges, seems more specific.

The U.S. sample had a significant positive correlation of Masculinity and leader Work-assignment scores that differed significantly from the Taiwanese correlation value. Masculinity also correlated significantly negatively with endorsement of Contingent Punishment and Participation among U.S. workers but not so with Taiwanese workers. The work assignment and participation results seem to go together to indicate an expectation of decisive orders from leaders among masculine Americans. Masculinity among Taiwanese seems to lack this association.

The correlation patterns between Paternalism and the leadership-behavior scales were also different between the U.S. and Taiwan. The correlation between Paternalism and Specification of Procedures was significantly higher for Taiwanese than that for Americans. Again, this fits with how this construct is normally defined. Those high in Paternalism should expect high-status others to control their work more closely. Higher Paternalism among Americans, though, was associated with expectations of more Supportive behavior and less use of Contingent Punishment. These differences seem to correspond to a link of Paternalism to socioemotional leadership among U.S. workers, but among Taiwanese it corresponds to task leadership. This should be tested more thoroughly and directly in future research. If it is accurate, it indicates a need to expand (or elaborate) the concept of paternalism.

Implications and Conclusions

The results of our study point toward several issues that need to be addressed in future research on cultural influences on leadership, as well as some potential applied implications for the management of cross-national workforces.

Limitations of and Directions for Future Research

The characteristics of the groups used in the study yield some external validity concerns. The national samples were selected to control for organization and job types. The trade-off is that this creates a concern about whether the findings can be generalized to other companies or professions; this needs to be established. The results here should be somewhat comparable to those of Hofstede (1980), however, since he also had subjects from high-technology firms. Despite the similarity in organization type and professions between our samples and Hofstede's U.S. and Taiwanese groups, we found some differences from Hofstede's results in value scores and their apparent impact. Thus, it seems clear that organization type and profession do not entirely overwhelm other influences in this type of research.

In future research, we need to examine how culturally shaped leadership ideals and how well leaders meet them, influence organizational and individual outcomes. To do this, we need to elaborate our models of how matches and mismatches in expectations and leader behavior influence outcomes. And, since we only examined reported ideals, not actual behaviors, research is needed that directly examines the behavior of individuals and the relationship between these and organizational outcomes. In addition, we have argued that organizational norms and policies may be more crucial than leader actions to the work behaviors of Taiwanese. We did not, however, directly assess norms, policies, and structure in this study. Cross-level studies that examine both individual-level variables, as we did here, and the organizational variables we simply speculated about are needed to provide stronger evidence on this point.

Moreover, it would clarify the nature of the cultural mechanisms to examine similarities and differences among the different subgroups within the U.S. and Taiwan on the patterns examined here and similarities and differences across groups that have common cultural heritages (e.g., U.S. workers of Anglo-Saxon descent with Anglo-Saxon Australians; Chinese-descent Taiwanese with those of Chinese descent in Singapore; see Khoo & James, 1994). Finally, we did not examine interactions of cultural variables with each other or with other social, organizational, and environmental circumstances. Such potential interactions need to be specified and examined in future research.

Applied Implications

Our results must be seen as tentative and in need of additional confirmation. Based on them, however, it would seem as if somewhat different approaches to leadership and motivation might be needed for Taiwanese and U.S. workers for greatest organizational effectiveness. On one hand, in line with our *Hypothesis 2b*, that Taiwanese will view leadership and motivational strategies as less important than U.S. workers, a more bureaucratic and normative approach might generally work better with Taiwanese workers. On the other hand, the actions of leaders and relations of supervisors and subordinates might generally have more impact on the work behaviors of U.S., as opposed to Taiwanese, workers.

In addition, there seem to be some differences concerning which specific leadership/motivation patterns will be most effective for these two national groups. In terms of House and Mitchell's four leadership styles (1974), a supportive leadership style and an achievement style may be more likely to be effective for U.S. workers than for Taiwanese. A directive leadership style, on the other hand, may be more effective with Taiwanese workers. Interestingly, no differences were found for the components of a participative approach. Means for both groups were relatively high for the scales tapping this approach, indicating that it may be fairly effective for both.

It is also the case that our research, and that of others such as Dorfman and Howell (1988), makes it seem possible to assess values at the individual level. Since different value orientations also seem to be related to differences in leader ideals, it might be possible to use value assessment to determine how best to manage each individual worker or which applicants to hire, given an organization's existing leadership and motivational systems.

The relatively high levels of Masculinity observed in our Taiwanese sample (as well as by Dorfman & Howell, 1988) may also have implications for U.S. MNCs operating in Taiwan and for Taiwanese MNCs operating in the U.S. Those in the U.S. may find that female managers and professionals will encounter more problems in dealings with local-national subordinates than their male counterparts. This would fit with anecdotal reports of generally greater sex-role stereotyping, female-male power and status differences, and sex bias in Taiwan. Taiwanese MNCs in the U.S. may similarly need to be on guard against any tendencies of their expatriate executives and managers to violate U.S. laws with policies and practices that are biased against the hiring, promotion, or other types of equal treatment of female managers and professionals. If, as we argued above, organizational norms and policies have more powerful effects among Taiwanese, it may be possible to counter any tendencies toward differential treatment of men and women by instituting strong norms and policies to the contrary.

Conclusions

Our study yielded some interesting preliminary results that may have important implications for theory and practice. Clearly, though, further theory development and related empirical work are needed to develop a solid understanding of how culture affects reactions to different approaches to leadership and motivation. Only then will we be positioned to confidently advise organizations about how to manage their multicultural workforces.

References

Beauvois, J.-L., & Dubois, N. (1988). The norm of internality in the explanation of psychological events. *European Journal of Social Psychology, 18*, 299-316.

Bhagat, R. S., Kedia, B. L., Crawford, S. E., & Kaplan, M. R. (1990). Cross-cultural issues in organizational psychology: Emergent trends and directions for research in the 1990s. In C. L. Cooper & I. T. Robertson (Eds.), *International review of industrial and organizational psychology* (Vol. 5, pp. 60-99). New York: Wiley.

Chang, S. K. C. (1985). American and Chinese managers in U.S. companies in Taiwan: A comparison. *California Management Review, 27*, 144-156.

Chen, D.-L. (1988). *A cross-cultural comparison of rules of working relationships.* Unpublished master's thesis, University of Kansas.

Cox, T. H., Jr. (1991). The multicultural organization. *Academy of Management Executive, 5*, 34-47.

Davis, H. J., & Rasool, S. A. (1988). Values research and managerial behavior: Implications for devising culturally consistent managerial styles. *Management International Review, 28*, 11-20.

Dorfman, P. W., & Howell, J. P. (1988). Dimensions of national culture and effective leadership patterns: Hofstede revisited. In R. N. Farmer & E. G. McGoun (Eds.), *Advances in international comparative management: A research annual* (Vol. 3, pp. 127-150). Greenwich, CT: JAI Press.

Dorfman, P. W., Howell, J., Cotton, C., & Tate, W. (1992). Leadership within the "discontinuous hierarchy" structure of the military: Are effective leadership behaviors similar within and across command structures? In K. E. Clark, M. B. Clark, & D. P. Campbell (Eds.), *Impact of leadership* (pp. 399-416). Greensboro, NC: Center for Creative Leadership.

French, J. R., Jr., & Raven, B. (1959). The basis of social power. In D. Cartwright (Ed.), *Studies in social power* (pp. 150-167). Ann Arbor, MI: University of Michigan Press.

Gudykunst, W. B., & Ting-Toomey, S. (1988). Culture and affective communication. *American Behavioral Scientist, 31*, 384-400.

Hinkin, T. R., & Schriesheim, C. A. (1989). Development and application of new scales to measure the French and Raven (1959) bases of social power. *Journal of Applied Psychology, 74*, 561-567.

Hofstede, G. (1980). *Culture's consequences.* Newbury Park, CA: Sage.

Hofstede, G., & Bond, M. H. (1984). Hofstede's culture dimensions: An independent validation using Rokeach's value survey. *Journal of Cross-cultural Psychology, 15*, 417-433.

House, R. J., & Mitchell, T. R. (1974). Path-goal theory of leadership. *Journal of Contemporary Business, 5*, 81-97.

Hsu, F. L. K. (1971). Psychosocial homeostasis and Jen: Conceptual tools for advancing psychological anthropology. *American Anthropologist, 73,* 23-44.

James, K. (1993a). The social context of organizational justice: Cultural, intergroup and structural effects on justice perceptions and behaviors. In R. Cropanzano (Ed.), *Justice in the workplace: Approaching fairness in human resource management* (pp. 21-50). Hillsdale, NJ: Erlbaum.

James, K. (1993b). Perceived self-relevance of technology as an influence on attitudes and information retention. *Journal of Applied Behavioral Science, 29,* 56-75.

Kanfer, R. (1990). Motivation theory and industrial/organizational psychology. In M. D. Dunnette & L. M. Hough (Eds.), *Handbook of industrial and organizational psychology* (2nd ed., Vol. 1, pp. 75-170). Palo Alto, CA: Consulting Psychologists Press.

Khoo, G., & James, K. (1994, April). *Issues, pitfalls, and methods of studying cultural influences on organizational outcomes: A model and example study.* Paper presented at the annual meeting of the Society for Industrial/Organizational Psychology, Nashville, TN.

Kotkin, J. (1993). *Tribes: How race, religion, and identity determine success in the new global economy.* New York: Random House.

Meindl, J. R., Hunt, R. G., & Lee, W. (1989). Individualism-collectivism and work values: Data from the United States, China, Taiwan, Korea, and Hong Kong. *Research in Personnel and Human Resources Management, 1* (Supplement A), 59-77.

Ng, S. H., Hossain, A. B., Ball, P., Bond, M. H., Hayashi, K., Lim, S. P., O'Driscoll, M. P., Sinha, D., & Yang, K. S. (1982). Human values in nine countries. In R. Rath, H. S. Asthana, D. Sinha, & J. B. H. Sinha (Eds.), *Diversity and unity in cross-cultural psychology.* Lisse, Netherlands: Swets and Zeitlinger.

Podsakoff, P. M., Dorfman, P. W., Howell, J. P., & Todor, W. D. (1986). Leader reward and punishment behaviors: A preliminary test of a culture-free style of leadership effectiveness. In R. Farmer (Ed.), *Advances in international comparative management: A research annual* (Vol. 2, pp. 95-138). Greenwich, CT: JAI Press.

Podsakoff, P. M., & Schriesheim, C. A. (1985). Field studies of French and Raven's bases of power: Critique, reanalysis, and suggestions for future research. *Psychological Bulletin, 97,* 387-411.

Rokeach, M. (1973). *The nature of human values.* New York: Free Press.

Rodrigues, C. A. (1990). The situation and national culture as contingencies for leadership behavior: Two conceptual models. In S. B. Prasad (Ed.), *Advances in international comparative management: A research annual* (Vol. 5, pp. 51-68). Greenwich, CT: JAI Press.

Ronen, S. (1986). *Comparative and multinational management.* New York: Wiley.

Schriesheim, C. A. (1978). *Development, validation, and application of new leader behavior and expectancy research instruments.* Unpublished doctoral dissertation, The Ohio State University.

Smith, P. B., & Bond, M. H. (1993). *Social psychology across cultures: Analysis and perspectives.* Needham Heights, MA: Allyn & Bacon.

Triandis, H. C. (1972). *The analysis of subjective culture.* New York: John Wiley.

Triandis, H. C. (1989a). The self and social behavior in differing cultural contexts. *Psychological Review, 96,* 506-520.

Triandis, H. C. (1989b). Cross-cultural studies of individualism and collectivism. In J. Berman (Ed.), *Nebraska Symposium on Motivation* (pp. 41-133). Lincoln, NE: University of Nebraska Press.

Uhl-Bien, M., Tierney, P. S., Graen, G. B., & Wakabayashi, M. (1990). Company paternalism and the hidden-investment process. *Group & Organization Studies, 15,* 414-430.

Wallace, A. F. C. (1971). *Culture and personality* (2nd ed.). New York: Random House.

Wright, J. W. (General Editor; 1994). *The universal almanac.* Kansas City, MO: Andrews & McMeel.

Yukl, G. (1989). Managerial leadership: A review of theory and research. *Journal of Management, 15,* 251-289.

THE EFFECT OF VALUE DIFFERENCES ON SOCIAL INTERACTION PROCESSES AND JOB OUTCOMES: IMPLICATIONS FOR MANAGING DIVERSITY

Michele J. Gelfand
Kristine M. Kuhn
Phanikiran Radhakrishnan

University of Illinois, Urbana-Champaign

Abstract

As a result of demographic changes and a changing international marketplace, organizations are becoming more concerned about how to manage a culturally diverse workforce. This paper contends that understanding the psychological processes and outcomes that are affected by cultural diversity is essential to managing diversity in organizations. To this end, a theoretical model that integrates aspects of subjective culture, selected social-interaction processes, and job-related outcomes was developed and tested. It specifically posits the relation between value incongruity, communication quality and attributional confidence, and job satisfaction and organizational withdrawal. To test these relations, data were collected from employee-supervisor pairs from a large organization located in the Eastern U.S. Structural equations modelling for observed variables (Jöreskog & Sörbom, 1989) was used to test the hypothesized model. The analysis demonstrated that the model fit the data well. Implications for research on cultural diversity and for integrating workers with differing value systems in organizations are discussed.

✳ ✳ ✳

As the twenty-first century approaches, businesses across the United States are becoming more concerned with how to manage a culturally diverse

This study was funded by the Center for Human Resource Management, University of Illinois, Urbana-Champaign. The authors would like to thank Dr. Harry Triandis for all of his advice and support during this project. We also would like to express our gratitude to Jill Fennell, Karin Lynn Lash, and Jean Shubert for assistance in data management.

workforce. In fact, managing diversity in the 1990s has replaced other buzzwords such as participative management from the 1980s, and is often mentioned as being among the top challenges to be faced in the coming years. Economic and demographic trends justify those concerns. In the last several decades, as world trade and global economic activity have grown exponentially, organizations have gone from being primarily domestic to international, multinational, and even global in strategy (Adler, 1990). Many American companies, such as Coca-Cola and Dow Chemical, now earn a majority of their profits in another country or countries (Adler, 1990). With these transitions, businesses are faced with the implications of cultural diversity, not only for marketing and production of goods in other cultures but also for the management of the interaction of people of many cultures within international settings.

Moreover, cultural diversity is increasing in U.S. domestic organizations, as shown in the landmark report, *Workforce 2000: Work and Workers for the 21st Century* (Johnston & Packer, 1987), which predicts that by the year 2000, the majority of new entrants into the labor market will be women (47%) and minorities (38%), while only 15% will be white males. To be sure, dealing with diversity is not a novel issue for U.S. managers. Almost from the founding of the country, ethnic and gender diversity have characterized the workforce. What is new about this modern diversity, however, is that managers will encounter diversity much more frequently and at higher levels, both inside and outside their organizations (Triandis, Kurowksi, & Gelfand, 1994).

Because of these changes, researchers and practitioners need to understand the effects of cultural diversity in organizations. Unfortunately, the desire for practical solutions has far surpassed the development of theory in this area. We contend that investigating the social-interaction processes that are affected by cultural diversity is essential to managing diversity in organizations. The main purpose of this paper is to develop and test a model linking cultural diversity, social-interaction processes, and job outcomes to better understand the impact that cultural diversity has in organizations.

Some Definitions

Cultural diversity. When researchers and practitioners speak of the increasing cultural diversity in the U.S. workforce, what do they mean? A perusal of the diversity literature demonstrates that most think of diversity in terms of differences in *demographic attributes* of employees. In this view, diversity is defined as differences in attributes such as age, ethnicity, sex, and race (e.g., Tsui & O'Reilly, 1989). Given that these are physical attributes and highly conspicuous, it is not surprising that they have been the focus of diversity research.

An alternative view of diversity is that it reflects the differing *psychological attributes* of employees. That is, employees bring a specific *subjective culture* to the workplace, or a "group's characteristic way of perceiving its social environment" (Triandis, 1972, p. 3). Subjective culture includes many interrelated elements, such as attitudes, categorizations, norms, roles, and values. These elements are shaped by the social, ecological, and political environment surrounding that specific group, which constitutes the resources available to the group, past reinforcements for specific behaviors, and the group's history (Triandis, 1972). Elements of subjective culture are transmitted from generation to generation through the process of socialization. Moreover, people with different demographic characteristics are likely to have differing psychological attributes. For instance, individuals of the same gender are often faced with similar social, economic, and political conditions and are likely to be socialized to share a common set of attitudes, values, role expectations, and so forth (Eagley, 1987; Radhakrishnan, Kuhn, & Gelfand, 1994).

Consistent with previous research by Triandis and his colleagues (Triandis, 1989; Triandis, McCusker, & Hui, 1990), values were chosen as one of the most important features of subjective culture in this study since they are generally less susceptible to temporal and situational effects, as compared to other aspects of subjective culture (Schwartz & Huismans, 1991; Uutela, 1991).

Human values. Human values can be construed as what people view as "good or bad, beautiful or ugly, clean or dirty, valuable or worthless, right or wrong, kind or cruel, just or unjust, and appropriate or inappropriate . . . (and as) mental programs that govern specific behavioral choices" (Lustig, 1988, p. 56). Values have also been defined as desirable goals which serve as guiding principles in people's lives (Kluckhohn, 1951; Schwartz, 1992). Explicit in both of these definitions is that people behave in ways which enable them to achieve their values.

Values are thought to have a pervasive effect on individuals (Ravlin & Meglino, 1987). In particular, values influence the social-perception process or the process by which one selects, evaluates, and organizes stimuli to provide meaning and understanding to external events (Singer, 1987). In other words, values frame assumptions of what is important and therefore influence the selection and interpretation of external stimuli. Additionally, because values are thought to be hierarchically organized in memory (Rokeach, 1973), individuals apply dominant values in interpreting stimuli and are likely to perceive implications for their own specific values across situations (Ravlin & Meglino, 1987).

Schwartz and his colleagues have developed a theory of specific values and universal relations among these values (Schwartz, 1992; Schwartz & Billsky, 1990). Based on 82 samples from 37 countries, they derived 10 value types from 56 specific values. Through smallest space analysis of the correlations among the importance ratings of these values (Guttman, 1968), Schwartz and Billsky (1990) found a circular structure of the relations among the value types. Figure 1 depicts the universal value structure that has been supported in these studies.

Figure 1. Theoretical Structure of Relations among Schwartz's Value Types

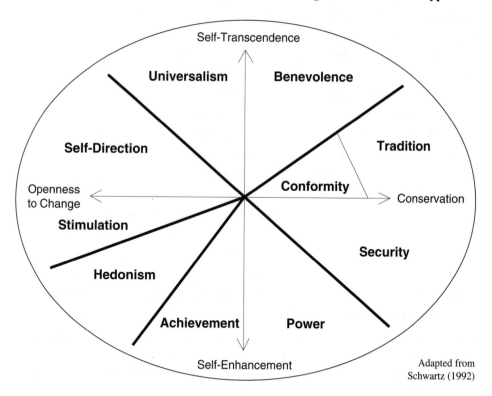

Adapted from
Schwartz (1992)

This circumplex of value types has two basic dimensions. The first contrasts a focus on conservation (indexed by the value types, tradition/conformity and security) with openness to change (indexed by the value types, stimulation and self-direction). The second dimension contrasts a focus on self-transcendence (indexed by the value types, benevolence and universalism) with self-enhancement (indexed by the value types, achievement and power; Triandis & Schwartz, 1993). Hedonism is related to both openness to change and to self-enhancement. A more complete description of these value types is provided in the Appendix (see p. 71).

According to Schwartz's theory, adjacent value types in the circumplex are theoretically compatible (e.g., tradition and security), whereas the remote value types are theoretically incompatible and likely to conflict (e.g., tradition and stimulation). In support of this, Schwartz (1992) found that, on average, the importance of theoretically compatible values varied together, while the importance of theoretically incompatible values varied inversely. The most severe conflict is likely to occur between individuals who place high importance on incompatible value types (Tetlock, 1986).

Effects of Value Differences in Organizations

Most relevant to this discussion are the effects of value differences, or *value incongruity*, on social-interaction processes and job outcomes in organizations. Much of the previous research has focused on the effect that value incongruity has directly on job outcomes (Meglino, Ravlin, & Adkins, 1989), and has generally found that value incongruity between supervisors and subordinates has a small negative correlation with job satisfaction and organizational commitment. However, little is known about what processes are affected by value incongruity among employees. It is posited here that value incongruity between employees affects two social-interaction processes: Communication and Attribution. Moreover, it is posited that these interaction processes are directly linked to job outcomes in organizations. These suppositions will be developed more fully below.

Value differences and communication processes. In any communicative encounter, there is a message sender and a message receiver. Messages sent are rarely identical to the messages received (Adler, 1990). A message sender encodes ideas into a symbolic representation or message, which may be in a verbal or nonverbal form. After the message has been sent through a channel, it reaches a receiver, who then must decode or attribute meaning to the symbolic ideas and behaviors and eventually respond through another encoded message (Adler, 1990). It is evident that the most successful communication will be one in which the participants of the interaction perceive and evaluate the message in terms of the intended idea or behavior.

Most pertinent to this discussion is that values can affect the perception and evaluation of external stimuli (Singer, 1987). Thus, employees who have different values may select different information from the environment and have disparate interpretations of the same encounter (Forgas, 1988). For instance, Forgas and Bond (1985) found that different values affected the interpretation of identical situations in Australia and Hong Kong. These cultures differ on the values of individualism and collectivism or the degree to which members of a culture emphasize independence or interdependence (Triandis, 1989). Australian students, who had more individualistic values, perceived situations in terms of freedom, competitiveness, and self-confidence, while Chinese students, with more collectivistic values, perceived the same situations in terms of communality and social usefulness.

Likewise in communicative encounters, we assert that the greater the differences in values between a sender and receiver, the greater the chance that they will construe the situation differently and will attach different meaning to the same words and behaviors. Consistent with this, Rogers and Bhowmik (1971) found that culturally heterogeneous groups who spoke the same language still suffered from delayed transmission of messages, message distortion, and restriction of communication channels. Although value differences were not assessed in this study, they may have contributed to the low quality of communication.

In sum, it is posited that when the sender of messages has different values from the receiver of the messages, the chances of accurately transmitting and interpreting messages as intended are lower than when the sender and receiver share the same values. Furthermore, since effective communication enhances coordination of activities between employees (Schein, 1985), employees who have high-quality communication with others should have higher job satisfaction. This is consistent with research on organizational communication, which has found a positive relationship between communication accuracy and job satisfaction (Muchinsky, 1977).

Value differences and attribution processes. Attribution processes refer to the way people come to understand why people behave the way they do. When people observe the behaviors of others, they make judgments about the causes of their behavior in order to understand, explain, and predict their behavior in various situations. Attributions can be retroactive, as in the case when people try to understand why others acted a certain way in the past. Attributions can also be proactive, as in the case when people try to predict how others will behave in future situations. The degree to which people are able to understand and predict how others will behave is referred to as *attributional confidence* (Gudykunst & Ting-Toomey, 1988). These processes are particularly important for the reduction of ambiguity and uncertainty in interactions in the workplace.

Value incongruity is likely to affect attributional confidence in organizations. As mentioned previously, values influence individuals' choice of behavior or broad modes of conduct (Kluckhohn, 1951). More specifically, values differ in the type of motivational goals that they direct, and people act in ways that may lead to the attainment of these goals across specific situations (Schwartz, 1992). As such, behaviors that are consistent with an individual's values are most likely to be seen as appropriate and endorsed in a given situation (Ravlin & Meglino, 1987). Consequently, employees who share similar values (i.e., have higher value congruity) may be better able to recognize the behavioral patterns of others and have the ability to predict their behavior in future situations (i.e., have greater attributional confidence). Although this has not been tested directly, differences in other aspects of subjective culture have been linked to attributional confidence. For instance, Gudykunst (1985) found that attitudinal similarity between students predicted attributional confidence in interactions between strangers. Presumably, attitude similarity reduces the number of alternative explanations for the behavior of others (Berger & Calabrese, 1975).

In this study, it was predicted that value incongruity among employees would relate to lower attributional confidence. Moreover, compared to employees with high attributional confidence, employees with low attributional confidence should experience more uncertainty and ambiguity in their interactions and lower job satisfaction (Adkins, Ravlin, & Meglino, 1992).

Summary: The Proposed Model

The proposed model in Figure 2 integrates aspects of subjective culture, selected social-interaction processes, and job outcomes among supervisor-employee pairs.

In this model, value differences between supervisors and employees are predicted to directly affect employees' perceived communication quality with supervisors, and employees' attributional confidence or ability to accurately predict supervisor behavior. We suggest that these processes, in turn, directly affect employees' job satisfaction. Moreover, based on research by Hanisch and Hulin (1990; 1991), job satisfaction is expected to be negatively related to organizational withdrawal behaviors.

Thus, several hypotheses were derived and tested from this conceptualization: (1) Higher levels of value congruity between supervisors and employees will be associated with higher levels of employees' perceived communication quality and attributional confidence; (2) higher levels of communication quality and attributional confidence will be related to higher job satisfaction; and (3) higher levels of job satisfaction will be related to lower levels of organizational withdrawal.

Figure 2. Proposed Model Relating Aspects of Subjective Culture to Social-interaction Processes and Job Outcomes

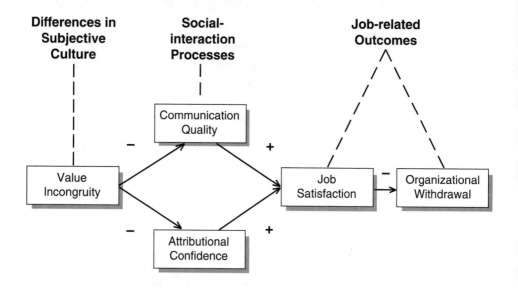

Method

Participants

Employees from a large organization located on the East Coast of the U.S. voluntarily participated in the study. A survey was distributed by administrators to 600 management employees from approximately 6 departments. All employees were from one of the top 3 levels in the organization (top management, employees supervised by top management, or subordinates of these employees). A total of 239 employees returned the completed questionnaires (40%).[1] The ethnic distribution of the respondents was 6 Native Americans, 157 Caucasians, 20 African-Americans, 22 Asian-Americans, and 9 Hispanics (25 respondents did not give this information). The median age of

---

[1] Phone calls were made to a subset of the original employees one month after the administration of the survey to identify reasons for not returning surveys. The primary reason for not returning the survey was a lack of time.

the sample was 47, and more than half (59%) had worked for the organization for more than 10 years. There were 180 males and 40 females in the sample (19 respondents did not give this information). From this sample, 98 supervisor-employee pairs were identified. There was, in fact, some overlap in the supervisor-employee pairs (e.g., there were some cases when one supervisor was included more than once in computing the congruity measure because of multiple employees). However, we have done additional analyses which have demonstrated that taking out this overlap *did not* change the relations among the variables. Thus, all of the pairs were included in the LISREL analysis.

Procedure

Two months prior to the survey administration, detailed lists of the supervisor-subordinate pairs in the top three levels of the entire organization were obtained. One week prior to the survey administration, a memo was circulated to employees informing them of the nature and purpose of the survey.

All surveys were distributed to employees by department administrators. Employees were asked to mail the completed survey to the University of Illinois in a stamped envelope provided. Employees were told that the survey was being conducted by researchers at the University of Illinois and that it was investigating what factors make people comfortable at work and satisfied with their jobs. They were also assured that all answers to the survey would be completely confidential. For research purposes, a number was placed on each survey in order to enable the classification of supervisor-subordinate pairs. Employees were told, however, that absolutely no information identifying individual responses would be related to anyone under any circumstances. A three-person research team from the University of Illinois remained on site for one week during the survey administration to answer any other questions about the project.

The Survey

The survey assessed the major components of the model.

Supervisor and Employee Values were assessed through a modified version of the Schwartz Value Scale (Schwartz & Billsky, 1990). For purposes of simplification and ease of administration, the 10 original value types shown in Figure 1 were collapsed to 8 by combining theoretically compatible value types (i.e., conformity and tradition, and self-direction and stimulation). The modified scale measures 32 specific values, which were chosen to reflect these 8 value types.[2] An explanation was given for each of the values to aid in interpretation. Individuals were asked to indicate how important these values were for them as guiding principles in their jobs, on a scale ranging from -1 (opposed to my values) to 7 (of supreme importance). For the purpose of reducing social desirability effects, employees were asked to not assign a rating of 7 to more than two values (Meglino, Ravlin, & Adkins, 1992). Cronbach alphas for each of the value types were all above .70, with the exception of security (alpha = .55). Based on item-total correlations, one of the specific values from this value type was excluded from the analysis.

Value incongruity was assessed by the sum of the absolute difference between the means of the 8 value types for each supervisor-employee pair. This measure was constructed based on Cronbach and Gleser's (1953) consideration of all possibilities for assessing congruency between two profiles. More specifically, Cronbach and Gleser (1953) suggest that the most appropriate technique to assess similarity between profiles is to analyze the linear distance between respective points in a *k*-dimensional space, where *k* is the number of clusters of variables included on an a priori grouping of items (Cronbach & Gleser, 1953, p. 472). In this study, the *k* clusters included were the value types, which were based on extensive analyses of the Schwartz Value Scale in 20 different countries (Schwartz, 1992; Schwartz & Billsky, 1990). As indicated previously, the items assessing these a priori value types were generally found to be internally consistent.

Communication quality was measured by items developed by the authors. Three items were designed to assess employees' perceived understanding of supervisors' communications: "It is difficult to figure out what my supervisor means"; "I can always understand my supervisor's point of view"; and "My supervisor always tries to make sure I understand what he/she is saying." All items were rated on 7-point Likert scales, ranging from strongly disagree to strongly agree. Cronbach's alpha for the communication quality index was .70.

Attributional confidence was measured by items developed by Gudykunst and Nishida (1986) and by items developed by the authors. Four items were designed to reflect employees' ability to predict various aspects of supervisor behavior: "How confident are you in your general ability to predict how he/she will behave?"; "How accurate are you at predicting his/her attitudes?"; "How accurate are you at predicting the values he/she holds?";

---

[2] The specific items can be obtained from the first author. Her address is: Department of Psychology, 6 Washington Place, New York University, New York, NY 10003-6634.

and "How confident are you in your ability to predict how he/she will act toward you on most days?" Items were scored based on a 1 (total uncertainty) to 5 (total certainty) scale. Cronbach's alpha for the scale was .87.

Job satisfaction was assessed by the Job Descriptive Index (JDI) (Smith, Kendall, & Hulin, 1969). This index measures the construct of job satisfaction with several scales, including satisfaction with work, satisfaction with pay, satisfaction with co-workers, and satisfaction with supervision. Two of these were chosen to be most relevant to the questions of interest in this study: satisfaction with work and satisfaction with supervision. The format of these questions asked individuals if their jobs or supervision had certain characteristics. Response options were "Yes," "No," or "?" (Unsure). Cronbach alphas for each scale were above .80. Since we were interested in the more general construct of job satisfaction, the scores for this variable were summed across the two scales for the analysis.

Organizational withdrawal was measured with a scale from Hanisch and Hulin (1990; 1991). Two interrelated aspects of employees' withdrawal were investigated in this study: work withdrawal, or those behaviors that serve to distance the employee from his or her work, such as being late or absent from work; and job withdrawal, or those behaviors that ultimately distance the employee from the organization itself, such as intention to quit. For these measures, employees rated on an 8-point scale how frequently they performed such behaviors. The Cronbach alpha for the entire scale was .77.

Analyses and Results

Table 1 provides descriptive statistics and the correlations for each of the variables in the model. The relations were tested simultaneously using structural equation modelling for observed variables (Jöreskog & Sörbom, 1989). In this analysis, a set of equations among the observed variables are estimated from a sample correlation matrix. Elements of the beta and gamma matrices were fixed (at zero) and freed (i.e., estimated) according to the postulated theoretical relations discussed in Figure 2. Maximum likelihood estimation was used to estimate the parameters. To identify the model, the diagonal of the psi matrix was fixed to unity.

The degree to which the model fit the sample data was examined next. Because different fit statistics are informative about alternative aspects of model fit, investigators typically examine a variety of measures for converging evidence of the quality of a solution. One common measure is the overall

Chi-Square statistic, which examines the hypothesis that the fitted model adequately describes the associations of the observed variables. The closer the obtained Chi-Square value is to its degrees of freedom, the better the fit of the hypothesized model. A general rule of thumb for an acceptable fit is if the ratio of the Chi-Square to its degrees of freedom is approximately 2.

Table 1. Descriptive Statistics and Correlations for the Variables in the Model

Variable	Mean	*SD*	1	2	3	4	5
1. Value Incongruity	8.75	3.71	1.00				
2. Communication Quality	15.17	3.39	-0.23	1.00			
3. Attributional Confidence	16.95	3.42	-0.20	0.36	1.00		
4. Job Satisfaction	37.98	9.97	-0.16	0.42	0.31	1.00	
5. Organizational Withdrawal	2.43	1.26	0.04	-0.20	-0.06	-0.47	1.00

However, because the Chi-Square statistic is dependent on sample size (and hence will usually lead to the rejection of any model when the sample is large), it is important to examine other indicators of fit as well. Typically, this includes the Root Mean Square Residual (RMSR), a measure of the magnitude of the differences between the fitted correlation matrix and the sample correlation matrix; the Goodness-of-fit Index (GFI) and the adjusted goodness of the fit (AGFI), which range between 0 and 1, although their exact statistical distributions are still unknown (Jöreskog & Sörbom, 1986); the standardized residuals; and the magnitude of the estimated beta and gamma coefficients between the observed variables. Together, these fit indices enable investigators to determine whether the model fits the data adequately.

The Chi-Square, RMSR, GFI, and AGFI statistics from the LISREL analysis are shown in Table 2. An examination of all of the fit statistics demonstrates that the model fit the data well. The Chi-Squared to degrees of freedom ratio was 2.3, the GFI was .95, AGFI was .87, and the RMSR was .08. Additionally, the standardized residuals were very small. Statistically, these results suggest that the relations among the observed variables are consistent with those postulated in Figure 2.

Table 2. Goodness-of-fit Indices for the Observed Model

Fit Statistic	Value
Chi-Squared	11.92
Degrees of Freedom	5
Chi-Squared to DF Ratio	2.31
Goodness-of-fit Index (GFI)	0.95
Adjusted Goodness of Fit (AGFI)	0.87
Root Mean Square Residual (RMSR)	0.08

Furthermore, all of the estimated beta and gamma coefficients of the model were significant at the .05 level, which is another indication of model fit. All of these coefficients had relatively small standard errors. The standardized coefficients are shown in Figure 3.

Figure 3. Beta and Gamma Coefficients of the Model Tested

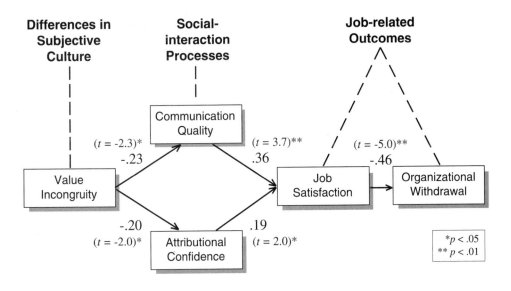

As the figure illustrates, the estimate of the path from actual value incongruity between employees and supervisors to communication quality was -.23. That is, actual value differences assessed through the Schwartz

Value Scale were negatively related to employees' perceptions of the quality of communication with supervisors. This is consistent with theory in cross-cultural psychology that predicts that value differences affect communication. The gamma coefficient from value incongruity to attributional confidence was -.20, supporting the notion that value differences impair one's ability to accurately predict another person's behavior.

The results also demonstrate that these social-interaction processes affect employees' job satisfaction. The path from communication quality to job satisfaction was .36, indicating that greater perceived communication quality was related to higher job satisfaction. The path from attributional confidence to job satisfaction was .19, indicating that greater attributional confidence concerning supervisor behavior was related to higher job satisfaction. Lastly, the path from job satisfaction to organizational withdrawal was -.46, strongly indicating that higher levels of job satisfaction were associated with lower levels of organizational withdrawal.

Discussion

The main purpose of this study was to examine how value differences affect social-interaction processes between employees and how these processes affect job-related outcomes. The fit statistics and the significant relations among the observed variables demonstrate that the proposed model fits the data well. More substantively, the results demonstrate that diversity, as measured by value differences, may hinder communication between employees and their supervisors and may affect employees' ability to predict their supervisors' behaviors. These processes in turn may lower job satisfaction and thereby enhance the likelihood of organizational withdrawal. This model, therefore, specifies the precise mechanism through which diversity may affect job-related outcomes in organizations.

Theoretical Implications

We suggest that research on cultural diversity in the workplace will benefit from studying how aspects of subjective culture affect social-interaction processes and job-related outcomes. Thus far, diversity research has concentrated on examining how demographic differences affect job outcomes (Jackson, Brett, Sessa, Cooper, Julin, & Peyronnin, 1991; Tsui, Egan, & O'Reilly, 1992). However, there is a lack of research that demonstrates the particular mechanisms through which demographics exert effects in organizations (for an exception, see O'Reilly, Caldwell, & Barnett, 1989). This study provides support for the argument that psychological attributes related to differences in subjective culture are related to social-interaction processes, such as communication and attribution.

Clearly, this paper does not examine all of the possible processes and outcomes that can be affected by differences in subjective culture. Future research should explore the effects of other aspects of subjective culture in organizations, such as differences in attitudes, categorizations, expectations, norms, roles, and self-construals (Triandis, 1972). It is also important to note that we examined only negative effects that differences in subjective culture can have on interaction processes and outcomes. Future research should examine the effect of differences in subjective culture on other social-interaction processes, such as creativity, to illuminate positive effects of diversity in organizations (Triandis et al., 1994). Furthermore, effects of subjective culture should also be examined at various levels of analysis, such as team, departmental, and organizational levels.

A more complete model of diversity will also include the context within which employees interact in organizations. As Triandis et al. (1994) indicate, in order to understand diversity, we must pay attention to the objective circumstances in which people have interacted, or the "culture of the relationship" that has developed over the centuries. This requires an analysis of the previous history of conflict, current power differentials, and reward systems, and how they contribute to differences in subjective culture, processes, and outcomes in organizations.

Lastly, because the data in this study were only cross-sectional, longitudinal research is still needed in order to establish causality between the processes and outcomes examined here.

Practical Implications

As stated previously, managers are becoming more concerned about how to manage a culturally diverse workforce. This study provides some insight into how organizations can manage the interaction of people of different cultures within domestic and international settings. In particular, it suggests that managers should examine the processes that are affected by differences in subjective culture, rather than focus on the differences in subjective culture per se. Once the processes are illuminated, interventions can be implemented to improve these interaction processes. For instance, in this study, value differences were shown to affect communication processes.

Rather than focus on the different values that employees hold, a more useful approach may be to focus on improving communication through training. This could be a particularly beneficial approach given that approximately 75% of the time is spent each day communicating with employees, either through writing, talking, or listening (Harris & Moran, 1981). Training could be designed to help employees understand how their values affect both verbal and nonverbal communication and how they can try to increase their communication accuracy by deciphering when miscommunications occur. Similarly, interventions can be targeted at reducing uncertainty and ambiguity in interactions by focusing on role-clarification and behaviors among supervisors and their employees. In sum, improving our understanding of communication processes may be very helpful in designing effective methods to manage diversity in organizations.

References

Adkins, C. L., Ravlin, E. C., & Meglino, B. M. (1992, August). *Value congruence between coworkers and its relationship to work-related outcomes.* Presented at the Academy of Management Annual Meeting, Las Vegas, NV.

Adler, N. J. (1990). *International dimensions of organizational behavior.* Boston: Kent Publishing Company.

Berger, C. R., & Calabrese, R. J. (1975). Some explorations in initial interactions and beyond: Toward a developmental theory of interpersonal communication. *Human Communication Research, 1,* 99-112.

Cronbach, L. J., & Gleser, G. C. (1953). Assessing similarity between profiles. *Psychological Bulletin, 6,* 456-473.

Eagley, A. H. (1987). *Sex differences in social behavior: A social role interpretation.* Hillsdale, NJ: Erlbaum.

Forgas, J. (1988). Episode representations in episode communication. In Y. Kim & W. Gudykunst (Eds.), *Theories in intercultural communication* (pp. 186-212). Beverly Hills, CA: Sage.

Forgas, J., & Bond, M. (1985). Cultural influences on the perception of interaction episodes. *Journal of Cross-Cultural Psychology, 11,* 75-88.

Gudykunst, W. (1985). The influence of cultural similarity, type of relationship, and self-monitoring on uncertainty reduction processes. *Communication Monographs, 52,* 203-217.

Gudykunst, W., & Nishida, T. (1986). Attributional confidence in low and high context cultures. *Human Communication Research, 12,* 525-549.

Gudykunst, W., & Ting-Toomey, S. (1988). *Culture and interpersonal communication.* Newbury Park, CA: Sage.

Guttman, L. (1968). A general nonmetric technique for finding the smallest coordinate space for a configuration of points. *Psychometrica, 33,* 469-506.

Hanisch, K. A., & Hulin, C. H. (1990). Job attitudes and organizational withdrawal: An examination of retirement and other voluntary withdrawal behaviors. *Journal of Vocational Behavior, 37*, 60-78.

Hanisch, K. A., & Hulin, C. H. (1991). General attitudes and organizational withdrawal: An evaluation of a causal model. *Journal of Vocational Behavior, 39*, 110-128.

Harris, P. R., & Moran, R. T. (1981). *Managing cultural differences*. Houston: Gulf Publishing.

Jackson, S. E., Brett, J. F., Sessa, V. I., Cooper, D. M., Julin, J. A., & Peyronnin, K. (1991). Some differences make a difference: Individual dissimilarity and group heterogeneity as correlates of recruitment, promotions, and turnover. *Journal of Applied Psychology, 76*, 675-689.

Johnston, W. B., & Packer, A. (1987). *Workforce 2000: Work and workers in the 21st century*. San Francisco: Jossey-Bass.

Jöreskog, K. G., & Sörbom, D. (1986). *LISREL VI: Analysis of linear structural relationships by maximum likelihood* (4th ed.). Mooresville, IN: Scientific Software, Inc.

Jöreskog, K. G., & Sörbom, D. (1989). *LISREL VII user's reference guide*. Mooresville, IN: Scientific Software, Inc.

Kluckhohn, C. (1951). Values and value-orientations in the theory of action. In T. Parsons & E. Shils (Eds.), *Toward a general theory of action* (pp. 388-433). Cambridge, MA: Harvard University Press.

Lustig, M. W. (1988). Value differences in intercultural communication. In L. A. Samovar & R. E. Porter (Eds.), *Intercultural communication: A reader* (pp. 55-61). Belmont, CA: Wadsworth.

Meglino, B. M., Ravlin, E. C., & Adkins, C. L. (1989). A work values approach to corporate culture: A field test of the value congruence process and its relationship to individual outcomes. *Journal of Applied Psychology, 74*, 424-432.

Meglino, B. M., Ravlin, E. C., & Adkins, C. L. (1992). The measurement of work value congruence: A field study comparison. *Journal of Management, 18*, 33-43.

Muchinsky, P. M. (1977). Organizational communication: Relationships to organizational climate and job satisfaction. *Academy of Management Journal, 20*(4), 592-607.

O'Reilly, C. A., Caldwell, D. F., & Barnett, W. P. (1989). Work group demography, social integration, and turnover. *Administrative Science Quarterly, 34*, 21-37.

Radhakrishnan, P., Kuhn, K., & Gelfand, M. J. (1994, July). *Workplace diversity: Its relation to value differences*. Paper presented at the 23rd International Congress of Applied Psychology, Madrid, Spain.

Ravlin, E. C., & Meglino, B. M. (1987). Issues in work values measurement. In W. C. Frederick (Ed.), *Research in corporate social performance and policy* (Vol. 9, pp. 153-183). Greenwich CT: JAI Press.

Rogers, E., & Bhowmik, D. K. (1971). Homophily-heterophily: Relational concepts for communication research. *Public Opinion Quarterly, 34*, 523-538.

Rokeach, M. (1973). *The nature of human values*. New York: Free Press.

Schein, E. H. (1985). *Organizational culture and leadership*. San Francisco: Jossey-Bass.

Schwartz, S. H. (1992). Universals in the content and structure of values: Theoretical advances and empirical tests in 20 countries. In M. Zanna (Ed.), *Advances in experimental social psychology* (Vol. 25, pp. 1-65). New York: Academic Press.

Schwartz, S. H., & Billsky, W. (1990). Toward a theory of universal content and structure of values: Extensions and cross-cultural replications. *Journal of Personality and Social Psychology, 58*, 878-891.

Schwartz, S. H., & Huismans, S. (1991). *Religiosity and value priorities: A study of Protestants, Catholics, and Jews*. Unpublished manuscript.

Singer, M. R. (1987). *Intercultural communication: A perceptual approach*. Englewood Cliffs, NJ: Prentice Hall.

Smith, P. C., Kendall, L., & Hulin, C. H. (1969). *The measurement of satisfaction in work and retirement*. Chicago: Rand McNally.

Tetlock, P. (1986). A value pluralism model of ideological reasoning. *Journal of Personality and Social Psychology, 50*(4), 819-827.

Triandis, H. C. (1972). *The analysis of subjective culture*. New York: John Wiley.

Triandis, H. C. (1989). The self and social behavior in differing cultural contexts. *Psychological Bulletin, 96*, 506-520.

Triandis, H. C., Kurowski, L. L., & Gelfand, M. J. (1994). Workplace diversity. In H. C. Triandis & M. D. Dunnette (Eds.), *Handbook of industrial and organizational psychology* (Vol. 4, pp. 769-827). Palo Alto, CA: Consulting Psychologists Press.

Triandis, H. C., McCusker, C., & Hui, C. H. (1990). Multimethod probes of individualism and collectivism. *Journal of Personality and Social Psychology, 59*, 1006-1020.

Triandis, H. C., & Schwartz, S. (1993). *Values, personality, and well-being*. Grant application to the Department of Human Services.

Tsui, A. S., Egan, T. D., & O'Reilly, C. A., III (1992). Being different: Relational demography and organizational attachment. *Administrative Science Quarterly, 37*, 549-579.

Tsui, A., & O'Reilly, C. A., III (1989). Beyond simple demographic effects: The importance of relational demography in superior-subordinate dyads. *Academy of Management Journal, 32*(2), 402-423.

Uutela, M. (1991). *Value priorities and political orientations across cultures*. Paper presented at the 2nd European Congress of Psychology, Budapest, Hungary.

Appendix

Definitions of Schwartz's (1992) Value Types

Power	Control or dominance over people and resources.
Achievement	Personal success through demonstrating competence.
Hedonism	Pleasure and gratification for oneself.
Stimulation	Excitement, novelty, and challenge in life.
Self-direction	Independent thought and action.
Universalism	Protection for the welfare of all people and for nature.
Benevolence	Enhancement of the welfare of people with whom one is in frequent contact.
Tradition	Respect for and acceptance of the time-honored customs.
Conformity	Restraint of actions likely to upset others or violate social norms.
Security	Safety, harmony, and stability of society, of relationships, and of self.

THE IMPACT OF
GROUP COMPOSITION

PERSONALITY DIVERSITY AND ITS RELATIONSHIP TO MANAGERIAL TEAM PRODUCTIVITY

Keith M. Eigel
Karl W. Kuhnert

Department of Psychology
University of Georgia

Abstract

In this study, we researched the effects of personality diversity and social-interaction processes on managerial team productivity. We studied 89 problem-solving teams, comprised of 476 managers, in a national retail chain. Results show that personality diversity in and of itself is not significantly related to team productivity. However, there is a significant interaction between personality diversity and the quality of team social-interaction processes (communication, trust, and openness). The findings indicate the importance of team personality composition and its effect on team productivity. Implications for future research are discussed.

✳ ✳ ✳

Today more than ever, organizations rely on teams to increase productivity (Buchholtz, Roth, & Hess, 1987; Dyer, 1987; Guzzo & Shea, 1992; Hirschhorn, 1991; Jackson & Associates, 1992; Ouchi, 1981; Peters & Waterman, 1982; Varney, 1989). Past research on teams has shown that cohesiveness (Seashore, 1954), reward and goal structures (Shea & Guzzo, 1987; Varney, 1989), and communication interaction (Hackman & Morris, 1975) are factors that contribute to productive work teams. Since publication of the Hudson report, *Workforce 2000: Work and Workers for the 21st Century* (Johnston & Packer, 1987), however, researchers have given a great deal of attention to the impact that diversity may have on team effectiveness (Cox, 1993; Jackson & Associates, 1992).

In the present study, research was conducted with managerial problem-solving teams, comprised of retail-outlet managers, to determine the impact of the personality diversity of teams and social-interaction processes (i.e., communication, trust, and openness) on one measure of team effectiveness: productivity.

The research reported here contributes to what is hoped will be a continually expanding body of empirical research that can increase knowledge, not only about the effects of diversity on productivity but also about the underlying organizational and social processes.

Factors Affecting Team Effectiveness

Research has shown linkages among managerial problem-solving team effectiveness and diversity of team composition, social-interaction processes, and the interaction of the two. This study explores these relationships, specifically examining the impact of personality diversity on team effectiveness.

Diversity

Diversity in the workplace has received considerable attention from researchers in the last decade, but work in the area actually goes back to the 1950s. Hoffman (1959) found that groups consisting of dissimilar personality profiles were more effective than homogeneous groups in terms of quality of solutions produced. Janis (1982) suggested that developing or structuring diversity among team members is a way of enhancing the quality of group decision making, and Guzzo (1986) stated that in problem-solving groups, it appears that maximizing diversity leads to increased productivity.

Since 1987, the pace of research on diversity has notably increased. This is partially a consequence of awareness of the Hudson report (Johnston & Packer, 1987), which illustrated the need to address diversity issues in organizations because of the changing demographic characteristics of the workforce. The authors pointed out that by the year 2000, white males will no longer constitute the majority of the workforce; rather, more than half will be women and minorities. This demographic information has generated writing on workplace diversity (i.e., Cox, 1993; Dyer, 1987; Jackson & Associates, 1992; Varney, 1989), focusing on the positive impact that diversity can have on team productivity. Even though much of the evidence presented in these writings is anecdotal and not empirical, it is consistent.

In his book on diversity in organizations, Cox (1993) stated that the potential creativity and problem-solving advantages gained by having a diverse workforce is a resource that remains grossly underutilized in most of the world. He contends that there is evidence that diversity may affect certain organizational processes that are closely related to performance. Many researchers argue that when diversity is properly managed, diverse groups and organizations have performance advantages over homogeneous ones (Copeland, 1988; Cox, Lobel, & McLeod, 1991; Esty, 1988; Mandell & Kohler-Gray, 1990; Marmer-Solomon, 1989). All of these individuals take the "value-in-diversity" (VID) perspective (Cox, 1993), which maintains that cultural diversity is an asset that organizations can use to enhance organizational performance.

Advocates of the VID perspective contend that diversity in work teams promotes creativity and innovation (Cox, 1993). In fact, many innovative companies deliberately create diverse teams in order to generate a multiplicity of points of view to confront problems (Kanter, 1983). Supporting this idea is the notion that a variety of perspectives can stimulate nonobvious alternatives (Nemeth, 1986). In her research, Nemeth showed that minority groups stimulated more solutions in a word-game problem than the majority group, and she concluded that persistent exposure to minority viewpoints stimulates creative thought processes. McLeod, Lobel, and Cox (1993) concluded that increased diversity will lead to higher levels of creativity and innovation (in Cox, 1993). Cox (1993) ended his chapter on diversity and its effect on productivity by saying:

> To the extent that organizations can attract, retain, and promote maximum utilization of people from diverse cultural backgrounds, they will gain competitive advantages in cost structures and in maintaining the highest-quality human resources. And, to the extent that organizations can capitalize on the potential benefits of cultural diversity in work groups, they will gain a competitive advantage in a) creativity, b) problem solving, and c) flexible adaptation to change. (p. 40)

Jackson and Alvarez (1992) also support the above ideas on diversity. They stated that when teams are formed, diversity is inevitable. Therefore, organizations that are able to meet the challenges associated with maintaining the best of the diverse workforce, are fair to those same workers, and create a synergistic team environment will be rewarded with greater workforce productivity and improved organizational health.

Diversity in the workplace has come to mean more than differences in race (Thomas, 1991). Jackson and Associates (1992) pointed out that the term *diversity* has grown to include variables such as sex, age, tenure, organizational culture, and personality. This study investigates specifically the relationship of personality diversity with the productivity of managerial problem-solving teams.

Personality Diversity

McGrath, Berdahl, and Arrow (1995) make the important point that diversity is not a generic term, and that the effects of diversity may change depending on whether one is speaking of demographic diversity, value diversity, status diversity, or personality diversity. Personality diversity in problem-solving groups is a diversity variable that can have an impact on team productivity.

Many instruments have been developed to assess personality type or preferences in individuals, and most can be used to distinguish levels of personality diversity in groups. The one chosen for this study, the Myers-Briggs Type Indicator (MBTI), measures preferences for styles of behavior that are relevant to communication styles, organizational problem solving, team-building, and conflict resolution (Hirsh & Kummerow, 1990). Responses reflect the following personality dimensions: Extraversion/Introversion, Sensing/Intuition, Thinking/Feeling, and Judging/Perceiving. The different patterns of scores on these dimensions can be organized into sixteen personality types. Differences in types and the specific combinations of these types on a team may be associated with problem-solving team effectiveness. (For more information on the MBTI, consult Hirsh & Kummerow, 1990, and Myers & McCaulley, 1985.)

Personality diversity may be an advantage to groups whose function it is to generate or improve procedures (McGrath et al., 1995). For instance, some managers have personality preferences for traditional stable environments, working in a step-by-step manner and contributing timely output. Others have preferences for troubleshooting, interactive learning, and the expeditious handling of the out-of-the-ordinary. Still others prefer visionary activities, ingenious and logical thinking, and strategy planning (Hirsh & Kummerow, 1990). One can easily see how a group of visionaries might have trouble bringing a solution to fruition, while a group of doers may have difficulty coming up with an innovative solution to work on.

Personality diversity in the context of problem-solving teams should benefit team effectiveness. This benefit is what Jackson and Alvarez (1992) call "the unleashing and taking full advantage of the latent potential of groups" (p. 27).

The conclusion of the writing and research to date leads one to believe that diversity in itself should lead to higher productivity and that personality diversity should lead to higher productivity, especially on problem-solving teams. Therefore, the first hypothesis is:

Hypothesis 1: Level of team personality diversity will be positively and significantly related to team productivity.

Interaction Processes (Communication, Trust, and Openness)

In addition to diversity, another important factor related to team effectiveness is the social-interaction process or how well the team functions as a unit (Dyer, 1987; Guzzo & Shea, 1992; Hirschhorn, 1991; Varney, 1989). The interaction process is defined by the levels of trust, openness, and communication exhibited by a team. Varney (1989) stated that organizations with good interaction processes allow dissent and disagreement to be dealt with through well-established and informal communication channels. Effective communication also requires openness and trust. Hirschhorn (1991) stated that trust and openness are prerequisites of effective communication, and the major response to the lack of these is that people stop communicating. According to Steiner (1972), when team members stop communicating there is interaction-process loss, which he defines as low levels of communication, trust, and openness.

Theoretically, developing higher levels of these interaction behaviors in teams should increase productivity. This belief is evidenced by the money spent by organizations on interventions aimed at developing favorable interaction processes, including, for example, discussions of how to deal with conflict. Such interventions assume that teams work best under the conditions of openness and trust that are created and developed by the intervention (Kaplan, 1979). One study that looked at the impact of a process intervention designed specifically to increase group-interaction processes found promising results related to team effectiveness (Sundstrom, De Meuse, & Futrell, 1990).

Hackman (1987; Hackman & Morris, 1975) and Steiner (1972) each developed models of how positive-interaction processes increase productivity. The first of these is the *input-process-output* model of team productivity. It posits that in certain types of groups, increasing interaction-process abilities enhances the input of group members. In this model, *input* refers to the things that group members bring to the group, including expertise, status, personality attributes, abilities, experience, and demographic attributes. *Process* refers to the interaction among group members, which includes social exchange, influence attempts, leadership efforts, and expressions of approval and disapproval. *Output* refers to the products yielded by the group or the productivity of the group (Guzzo & Shea, 1992).

Steiner (1972) developed a model that defines the impact of interaction process in terms of process loss. The model—*Actual productivity = potential productivity – process loss*—defines *potential productivity* as the highest level of performance attainable by the group and is determined by the available resources within a group (i.e., personnel, abilities, resources). *Actual productivity* fails to meet potential productivity because of process loss. *Process loss* is a result of less than optimal ways of combining members' resources, and could include things like missed communication and low motivation (Guzzo & Shea, 1992). Both models underscore the importance of the contribution of the interaction process to team productivity.

For the purposes of this study, the interaction process variable, consisting of communication, trust, and openness, is referred to as the *Quality-of-Interaction Process* or QIP. It is proposed that the higher the QIP the more productive the team will be. Support for this hypothesis confirms both of the preceding process models.

Hypothesis 2: QIP will be positively and significantly related to team productivity.

The Interaction of Diversity with QIP (Quality-of-Interaction Process)

Thus far, we have presented arguments that both personality diversity and QIP contribute to problem-solving team productivity. However, there is also evidence that these two factors interact to affect productivity. In a study of culturally diverse work teams, Adler (1986) showed that some of the culturally diverse teams were more productive than homogeneous teams, but that some were less productive. Cox (1993) interpreted this as evidence that, when teams manage diversity well (i.e., communication and openness are handled appropriately, and conflict issues are dealt with successfully), their diversity is an asset to performance, but when diversity is not managed well it detracts from performance.

McGrath and his colleagues (1995) supported the idea that the effectiveness of diversity depends on the context and management of it. They concluded that diversity of relevant personality characteristics may benefit a group's activities, provided the group members can communicate effectively enough to take advantage of their diverse perspectives. However, the effects will depend on the particular attribute, the type of group task, and other features of the group context (McGrath et al., 1995). In other words, we may not be able to make predictions about personality diversity in and of itself, but instead, predictions must be made contingent on the level of other pertinent variables such as QIP.

To put this in the context of Hackman's (1987; Hackman & Morris, 1975) input-process-output model: In problem-solving groups, personality diversity increases the available input, but the process variable (QIP) can moderate the effect that diversity has on output (productivity). However, there is also research that indicates that diverse groups sometimes perform worse than homogeneous groups because of incompatibility (Hill, 1982). This, combined with the information presented by Cox (1993) that poorly managed diversity can be a performance detractor, indicates that if process (QIP) is low, diverse groups will be less productive than homogeneous groups. Therefore, as stated earlier, it appears that staffing groups in a way that maximizes group diversity contributes to performance in problem solving and decision making (Guzzo, 1986) but only when QIP is high. More specifically—high-diversity teams would be effective only when QIP is high.

Steiner's (1972) model lends further support to the idea that group diversity's effect on productivity depends on the level of QIP:

Actual productivity = potential productivity – process loss

In the context of diverse group membership, this model proposes that what is potentially available to the group based on member contribution is decreased by process loss. Therefore, if process, or QIP, is high, process loss should be lowered, thereby increasing productivity. Since potential productivity brought to the group by diverse attributes appears to contribute to team effectiveness in problem-solving groups (Guzzo, 1986), high diversity and high QIP, according to Steiner's model, should sum to higher productivity. This interaction is illustrated in Figure 1 (p. 82).

It is proposed that the relationship of diversity to productivity will be attenuated by extreme group homogeneity and amplified by extreme group heterogeneity.

Therefore the third hypothesis of this study is:

Hypothesis 3: Diversity and QIP will interact; specifically, diverse personality teams will be more productive than non-diverse personality teams in high QIP environments but less productive in low QIP environments.

**Figure 1. Proposed Relationship Between Diversity and QIP
as It Relates to Productivity**

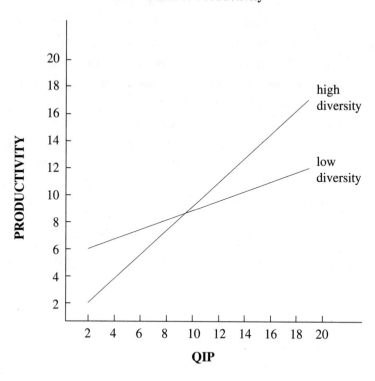

Method

Subjects

The managers. The sample was composed of 476 managers, each of whom was responsible for one retail location. Most managers were white (92.6%) and male (90.8%). All sixteen MBTI personality types were represented, but the distribution was uneven, with 34.9% classified as the same type. The mean age was 37.2 ($SD = 9.4$) and mean tenure was 7.6 years ($SD = 5.3$). (See the Appendix, p. 97, for complete demographic information.)

The organization assigned the managers to teams based on regional proximity. It is important to note, because of the relative homogeneity of the sample, that there was no systematic placement of any of the managers according to demographic categories or personality categories. The 476 managers made up 89 teams with a mean of 5.35 members per team ($SD = 1.96$). Each team was led by one of 24 trained team facilitators, each of whom had from two to five teams to lead. The teams met monthly, maintained fairly static membership, and had been meeting for over one year at the time the study was conducted.

The facilitators. The 24 team facilitators were employed by the organization. They had received approximately 12 days of training in group facilitation, problem-solving techniques, and a variety of exercises that dealt with general principles of team-building but not with specific issues of diversity. One potential problem recognized by the organization was the lack of reinforcement provided to the facilitators to follow up the training program.

The organization perceived the role of the facilitator to be that of a leader initially and then that of a facilitator as the team matures. During the start-up period, the facilitators played a very active role in the team process. Their participation was much like that of a T-ball coach who participates on the field with the young baseball players. As the team moved from the T-ball stage to the Little-League stage, if you will, the role of the facilitator turned to that of coach where he or she guided the team from the sidelines, rather than as an on-field participant.

The primary influence that the facilitator had over the managers was the ability to recommend to the organization that a manager be removed from the organization. The managers perceived this level of power and responded to the facilitator accordingly. The facilitator otherwise had no financial clout over team members. The organization described the facilitator's role as "a lot of selling, not much telling."

The teams. The purpose of the management teams in this organization was to solve problems that arose at the managers' retail locations. Most of the problems were operational issues, such as how to better contain inventory costs, how to contain labor costs, and how to increase sales on higher profitability products. Sometimes stores dealt with personnel problems at a particular manager's location, but this was the exception rather than the rule. Therefore, teams that solved problems most effectively should see increases in the productivity of individual outlets, thereby increasing the aggregated team score.

The increase in profitability of each store was the primary incentive for increasing team performance. Each manager's individual earnings were tied directly to the profitability of his or her store, hence the motivation for each manager contributing to the team process. Managers were awarded their retail outlet under the conditions of a semifranchise type of system. This meant that the manager was, in essence, running his or her own business. However, the parent organization had the ultimate right to the outlet and could dismiss managers or pull an outlet from them for a variety of poor-performance reasons.

In addition to tying earnings to profitability, the organization used recognition incentives to motivate team performance. Under this system the team members were recognized with a plaque or trophy, signifying exceptional team performance, at the annual meeting of managers sponsored by the corporate office.

The members were assigned to teams based on the sole criteria of regional proximity. There was only one instance where a team asked to have a member removed because of incompatibility. Accounting for this one exception, team membership remained almost completely stable, with the rare exception of a team member retiring or otherwise leaving the organization.

The organization was looking to the teams for effective problem solving. This, they believed, would increase individual store productivity, thereby increasing productivity across the whole organization.

Measures

Personality. Personality was assessed using the Myers-Briggs Type Indicator. This information was gathered from the personnel department of the organization. The MBTI is a forced-choice, self-report inventory based on Jung's theory of conscious psychological type (Willis, 1985) that assesses preferences for four personality dimensions: Extraversion/Introversion, Sensing/Intuition, Thinking/Feeling, and Judging/Perceiving. Scores on these dimensions can be used to classify people into sixteen different personality types.

The development of the MBTI is framed in both theoretical and empirical (statistical) methods (Willis, 1985) and satisfies many of the criteria of psychological tests (Devito, 1985). When examined for test-retest reliability, the forced-choice preference scores (or type-category scores) for the four dimensions produced phi coefficients ranging from .43 to .84. When category scores are converted to bimodal continuous scores, the test-retest reliability ranges from .69 to .84 for the four dimensions. The estimates of the continuous scores retain data precision lost in the use of the type-category scores, which accounts for the difference in reliabilities obtained from the two data types (Willis, 1985). Stability in the type-category scores has been reported using test-retest intervals up to six years, and the proportion of reclassification into three of the four preference classifications is 70% to 88% (McCaulley, 1981).

MBTI scores were not available for 135 of the 476 managers. However, the managers with missing scores were distributed nonsystematically across the teams. Any team missing scores from more than 50% of the managers

was not considered in the analysis. Therefore, 77 of the 89 teams were utilized in the personality-diversity analysis.

For the calculation of personality diversity based on MBTI scores,
Blau's (1977) index of heterogeneity for categorical variables was
computed by:

$$Heterogeneity = (1 - \Sigma pi^2)$$

where *p* is the proportion of group members in a category and *i* is the number
of different categories. The scale ranges from a low of 0 (no diversity) to a
theoretical high of 1.0 (Jackson, Brett, Sessa, Cooper, Julin, & Peyronnin,
1991).

QIP. The QIP (Quality-of-Interaction Process) measure is based on
items relating to communication, trust, and openness. The evaluation was
made by the team facilitators and was measured by 5 items on a 5-point
Likert scale; 1 represented 0% agreement with the statement and 5 repre-
sented 100% agreement. The 5 items were:
  • The team resolves conflict among its members effectively.
  • Trust is exhibited among team members.
  • Communication and feedback is open and honest.
  • The team atmosphere is supportive and encouraging.
  • The teams' actions demonstrate a concern for the success of each
    other.
The measures yielded a Cronbach alpha coefficient of .89.

Productivity. Productivity and effectiveness are terms that are often
confused in the literature (see Author Notes, p. 98). Pritchard (1992) and
Gladstein (1984) stress the importance of criterion measures that reflect the
measures the organization uses in the analysis of organizational productivity.
For this study, productivity was based on net income, profit, and customer
satisfaction. This measure was developed by the organization, and has been
used in the analyses of team performance since the inception of teams in the
organization.

The productivity measure was calculated by aggregating at the team
level the percent sales change, percent profit change, and a percent change in
customer satisfaction, all over the previous year. The results of each of these
percent changes were matched to a 5-point Likert scale, with 1 being the
lowest level of performance and 5 being the highest. The summary index
ranged, in theory, from 1 to 20, with 1 representing the lowest level of perfor-

mance and 20 representing maximum performance. The actual productivity
scores ranged from 1 to 17 with a mean of 8.2 and a standard deviation of 3.1.

Results

Table 1 provides descriptive data for the variables. There were 89 teams
used in the analysis of QIP on productivity (*Hypothesis 2,* p. 80). Only 77
teams met the study's criteria for the analysis of personality diversity and
personality diversity x QIP interaction on team productivity (*Hypotheses 1*
and *3* respectively, pp. 79 and 81).

Table 1. Means, Standard Deviations, and Correlations of Variables

Variable	Productivity	QIP	Per. Div.	No. on Team	*M*	*SD*
Productivity	1.00				8.20	3.10
QIP	.29*	1.00			13.05	3.64
Personality Diversity	-.11	-.06	1.00		.74	.13
Number on Team	-.02	-.15	.42*	1.00	5.35	1.96

* *p* < .01; *N* for QIP = 89; *N* for Personality Diversity = 77.

Table 1 also shows the correlation matrix of the analyzed variables, and
indicates that only QIP is correlated significantly with productivity (*p* < .01).

The number of team members, although correlated significantly with
personality diversity, had no significant relationship with productivity when it
was regressed on productivity, or when QIP x number of team-member
interactions was regressed on productivity.

The Diversity Hypothesis

As stated in *Hypothesis 1* (team personality diversity will be positively
and significantly related to team productivity), we expected to find a positive
relationship between diversity and productivity. Table 2, which contains the
results of the regression analysis for *Hypothesis 1* shows that personality
diversity is not, in and of itself, related to team productivity.

**Table 2. Regression Analysis Results Showing the Effect of
Personality Diversity on Productivity**

Variable	Coefficient	Standard error	*t*-value
Personality Diversity	-2.71	2.96	-.92
Intercept	10.35	2.22	4.67**

$N = 77$; $R^2 = .01$, Adjusted $R^2 = .002$; $F = .36**$.
* $p < .01$

The QIP Hypothesis

Hypothesis 2 predicted that QIP would be positively and significantly related to team productivity. As seen in Table 3 the data supported this hypothesis. There was a significant effect ($t < 2.76$; $p < .01$) for the regression of QIP on productivity with an adjusted $R^2 = .07$. It appears that QIP is a significant predictor of team productivity.

Table 3. Regression Analysis Results Showing the Effect of QIP on Productivity

Variable	Coefficient	Standard error	*t*-value
QIP	.25	.09	2.76**
Intercept	4.93	1.23	4.02

$N = 89$; $R^2 = .08$, Adjusted $R^2 = .07$; $F = 7.60**$.
* $p < .01$

The Interaction Hypothesis

Hypothesis 3 predicted that diverse personality teams would be more productive than non-diverse personality teams in high QIP environments but less productive in low QIP environments. That is, we expected to find an interaction between diversity and QIP. We found that the QIP x personality diversity interaction was significant ($t = -2.97$; $p < .01$) with an adjusted $R^2 = .15$, as shown in Table 4.

Table 4. Regression Analysis Showing the Effects of
QIP x Personality on Productivity

Variable	Coefficient	Standard error	*t*-value
Personality Diversity	39.06	14.18	2.76**
QIP	2.45	.75	3.27**
QIP x Personality Div.	-3.00	1.01	-2.97**
Intercept	-23.62	10.53	-2.24

$N = 77$; $R^2 = .18$, Adjusted $R^2 = .15$; $F = 5.30$**.
* $p < .01$

However, as seen in Figure 2, the interaction is opposite of what was predicted. QIP does in fact moderate the impact of personality diversity on team productivity, but the predicted effect was that high QIP would amplify the relationship of personality diversity on the most diverse teams and attenu-

Figure 2. The Effect of High versus Low Team Personality Diversity on the
Relationship Between QIP and Productivity

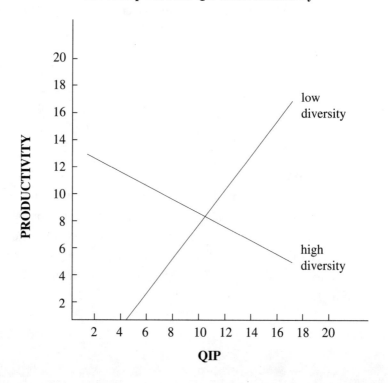

ate it on the most homogeneous teams (see Figure 1). The relationship found in this organization is dramatically different from the predicted effect and seems to go against both Steiner's (1972) and Hackman's (1987; Hackman & Morris, 1975) group-process models.

As seen from the graphic representation of the interaction in Figure 2, it appears that in this organization, level of productivity was positively related to the level of QIP on homogeneous teams. However, in the more diverse teams, QIP not only attenuated the expected relationship but, in fact, reversed the expected relationship.

Discussion

Because of the nature of the results of this study, it is appropriate to discuss the significance of the interaction hypothesis findings first, and then the impact of QIP and diversity as independent variables within the context of the interaction.

The Interaction Hypothesis

Based on the existing team and diversity literature, we expected to confirm the interaction hypothesis. That is, we expected to see high QIP (high trust, communication, and openness) amplify the positive relationship between personality diversity and productivity. We found exactly the opposite. As QIP increased, diverse teams became less productive and homogeneous teams became more productive (see Figure 2). In fact, when QIP was the lowest, the high-diversity teams had relatively high productivity. However, if increasing personality diversity actually detracts from productivity, we would expect to find a negative relationship between personality diversity and productivity (independent of QIP), which we did not.

In contrast, when diversity was low, we found a positive relationship between QIP and productivity. This is the expected relationship for QIP and productivity independent of diversity (i.e., as QIP increases on a team of similar members, so does productivity). What appears to happen in this sample is that the QIP effect is so strong for teams that have low personality diversity that it accounts for the confirmation of *Hypothesis 2* (QIP will be positively related to team productivity regardless of diversity).

Therefore, the QIP effect is so strong on homogeneous teams that even though it is related negatively to productivity on diverse teams, the analysis of QIP and productivity independent of diversity still shows QIP and productivity being positively related. For this reason, the findings of the first two hypotheses (the diversity and QIP hypotheses) should not be discussed outside the context of the interaction hypothesis.

Because past research and theory on diversity, QIP, and teams was not supported by the findings of our research, we searched for plausible explanations as to why this was the case. We derived two related explanations, which were confirmed by the executive members of the subject organization when the findings of the study were presented to them. One explanation has to do with the dominant personality type at the organization and the other has to do with the company culture. In addition, the organization was able to provide illustrations which support these explanations.

A dominant personality type may have an effect on group process. Our findings suggest that perhaps the presence of a dominant personality type influenced the group process of the organization and, therefore, the findings of the study. Not only are the majority of these managers white males (see Appendix), but they are also overwhelmingly one of two very similar MBTI types: ESTJ (Extraversion, Sensing, Thinking, Judging) and ISTJ (Introversion, Sensing, Thinking, Judging). These two types represent the personality preferences of over 45% of the managers. (The remaining 14 types measured by the MBTI account for the remainder of the sample.) Although these two types have many strengths, they also have some characteristics that may cause them to respond negatively to team diversity.

As far as their strengths are concerned, ESTJs generally have the ability to see flaws in advance, critique problems logically, monitor effectively, and follow through on projects in a step-by-step manner. They are task oriented, organized, structured, stable, efficient, and goal oriented. ESTJs are a particularly good fit with the managerial job studied here, because many of the responsibilities managers have at their individual locations are the same, day after day. Therefore, personality characteristics like efficiency, structure, and organization are assets to performance. In addition, the organization has traditionally set performance goals in a way that favors goal-oriented managers with good monitoring skills, which are strengths of ESTJs.

However, some of these strengths may manifest themselves as problems for team functioning. ESTJs seek leadership and take charge quickly; they solve problems quickly but usually based only on past experience; they are often too quick to decide; and they are most comfortable functioning in hierarchical situations (perhaps the antithesis of the team concept). In addition, ESTJs have a preference for overlooking niceties in order to get the job done (Hirsh & Kummerow, 1990). Thus, it may be very hard for other types to work with them.

ISTJs have many of the same skills to offer this organization as ESTJs but in a more introverted style. They prefer stability, schedules, goals, structure, and honoring commitments. They respect hierarchical structures and prefer to function in them, but they do not seek leadership positions the way ESTJs do. However, like ESTJs, they tend to overlook interpersonal niceties in order to get the job done, and they also may become rigid in their ways and be thought of as inflexible (Hirsh & Kummerow, 1990). The same problem-solving benefits added by the diverse team, as discussed above, are not preferred modes of operation for ISTJs either. They need to become more open to wide ranges of solutions to problems, and they may need to try fresh alternatives to avoid getting in "working ruts" (Hirsh & Kummerow, 1990).

As previously stated, over 45% of the managers in this organization fall into the two personality preferences described above, types which we believe are unlikely to appreciate diversity in personality styles. ESTJs and ISTJs tend to steamroll other personality types, and thereby squelch their ideas in problem-solving settings.

The director of teams from the organization studied here illustrates how this can take place. In one team setting, a problem was presented to the group. Several of the ESTJ team members quickly analyzed it and presented a solution that had worked in their own retail locations (a classic characteristic of ESTJs). They tried to quell any further input on the subject, because from their perspective the problem had been identified and solved; it was time to move to the next challenge. Only because the director was there were they willing to spend additional time talking about other possible solutions. They then reluctantly agreed to commit to collecting data concerning the problem, which could be analyzed at the next meeting. However, the director agreed that his influence was the primary reason that the process continued to this point, and he was aware that this may not have occurred had he not been present.

This illustrates how ESTJ-dominant teams may function in an organization, and how diversity, even personality diversity, may not be valued or utilized in the problem-solving tasks presented to teams with a strong ESTJ-dominant culture. In order to analyze this effect, we did a post-hoc analysis of the organization, removing the ESTJ-dominant teams (defined as having more than 50% of the team members as ESTJs) from the analysis. This took away about 30 teams, leaving us with 53 teams. The post-hoc analysis illustrated that there was an "ESTJ effect," but it did not give clear support for the explanation just presented.

When ESTJ-dominant teams were removed, there was no significant interaction effect at all. However, the correlation between QIP and team productivity (the QIP hypothesis) was no longer significant, either. This could mean that, when QIP is high on ESTJ-homogeneous teams, productivity is high. High trust and openness, along with effective communication (characteristics of high QIP teams) leads to effective problem solving on these teams, while low QIP detracts from the ESTJ-dominant team's performance.

This notion of ESTJ dominance as the main reason for the unusual interaction findings is further confirmed by the fact that in the post-hoc analysis, with the ESTJ-dominant teams removed, personality diversity has a significant negative relationship with team productivity ($p < .05$). This means that the more diverse the remaining teams, the lower their productivity is independent of QIP. That is, there is a significant negative relationship between personality diversity and productivity in the post-hoc analysis.

The organization may not value personality diversity. A possible second explanation for these findings is the possibility that this organization has a culture that does not value personality diversity. We suggest that because of an inability or unwillingness to value personality diversity, the number of solutions organizational members can avail themselves of when problems occur in team settings may be limited.

For instance, organizational members know from past research that ESTJ managers are traditionally successful. Therefore, they believe that the 30 ESTJ-dominant teams may solve problems more effectively than non-ESTJ-dominant teams, and this ability to solve problems effectively may improve as QIP goes up. All team members hold the same job and the ESTJ type fits the demands of the job well, which leads us to believe that the effectiveness of these teams may be because their members are well-suited to their occupation. This conjecture is supported by the post-hoc findings.

However, the remaining 53 non-ESTJ-dominant teams may not have the same skill set, which comes so naturally to ESTJs, with which to solve problems specific to this organization. Therefore, when they are teamed up in an organization whose culture does not value personality diversity (rather it prefers ESTJ-type methods for solving problems), then the result is that as diversity among these team members increases, the ability to effectively solve problems decreases. Thus, by diminishing the contributions of non-ESTJs, the organization finds that team effectiveness and productivity are ultimately affected.

In the context of this explanation, we suggest that non-ESTJ-dominant teams are restricted in their ability to benefit from diversity because it is not valued in their organizational culture. This explanation is consistent with Schneider's (1987) attraction, selection, attrition (ASA) framework, which suggests that organizations attract a homogeneous population and that people who don't fit deselect and leave. Thus, organizational cultures reinforce the behavior of dominant types.

According to the director of teams for this organization, an implication of both of the above explanations is that the organization could be in danger of losing ground to the competition because of the homogeneity of personality types among managers. ESTJs are set in their ways and like stability and structure. Because the retail market they are in is changing rapidly, there is a feeling that ESTJ dominance may not benefit them as much as it has in the past. Therefore, there is a need to diversify the personality types of the store managers in order to meet the demands of the changing environment.

Implications

This study challenges the existing body of diversity research. However, we do not believe that the findings presented here illustrate lack of value in personality diversity. Rather, we believe that personality diversity must be properly managed in order for it to positively affect productivity. In this company, diversity of personality style was unattended to. In addition, QIP must be properly developed, and the organization must create a culture that values diversity if it indeed plans to utilize the benefits potentially created by diverse team composition.

Future research should focus on the particular personality composition of teams, rather than just the level of personality diversity. We will learn through this type of analysis how personality diversity, when structured effectively, can benefit organizations greatly. If the strengths of each personality type are known in the context of how they contribute to a particular organization, we can utilize this in team problem solving to positively influence the level of productivity that the teams are able to achieve.

The organization studied here believes that there is value in personality diversity, and efforts are being made to improve the team process by intentionally allowing non-ESTJ perspectives to be voiced and considered. We believe that these efforts will lead to increased productivity in this organization, and that these lessons have implications for other organizations as well.

References

Adler, N. (1986). *International dimensions of organizational behavior.* Boston: Kent Publishing.

Blau, P. M. (1977). *Inequality and heterogeneity.* New York: Free Press.

Buchholtz, S., Roth, T., & Hess, K. (1987). *Creating the high performance team.* New York: John Wiley & Sons.

Copeland, L. (1988, June). Valuing workplace diversity. *Personnel,* pp. 52-60.

Cox, T. H. (1993). *Cultural diversity in organizations: Theory, research, and practice.* San Francisco: Berrett-Koehler.

Cox, T. H., Lobel, S., & McLeod, P. (1991). Effects of ethnic group cultural difference on cooperative versus competitive behavior in group task. *Academy of Management Journal, 34,* 827-847.

Devito, A. J. (1985). Review of the Myers-Briggs Type Indicator. In J. V. Mitchell (Ed.), *Buros, the ninth mental measurements yearbook* (pp. 1030-1032). Lincoln, NE: The University of Nebraska Press.

Dyer, W. G. (1987). *Team building: Issues and alternatives* (2nd ed.). Reading MA: Addison-Wesley.

Esty, K. (1988). Diversity is good for business. *Executive Excellence, 5,* 726-749.

Gladstein, D. (1984). Groups in context: A model of task group effectiveness. *Administrative Science Quarterly, 29,* 499-517.

Guzzo, R. A. (1986). Group decision making and group effectiveness in organizations. In P. S. Goodman (Ed.), *Designing effective work groups* (pp. 34-71). San Francisco: Jossey-Bass.

Guzzo, R. A., & Shea, G. P. (1992). Group performance and intergroup relations in organizations. In M. D. Dunnette (Ed.), *Handbook of industrial/organizational psychology* (2nd ed., Vol. 4, pp. 269-307). Palo Alto, CA: Consulting Psychologists Press.

Hackman, J. R. (1987). The design of work teams. In J. W. Lorsch (Ed.), *Handbook of organizational behavior* (pp. 315-342). Englewood Cliffs, NJ: Prentice Hall.

Hackman, J. R., & Morris, C. G. (1975). Group tasks, group interaction process, and group performance effectiveness: A review and proposed integration. In L. W. Berkowitz (Ed.), *Advances in experimental social psychology* (Vol. 8). New York: Academic Press.

Hill, M. (1982). Group versus individual performance. Are N + 1 heads better than one? *Psychological Bulletin, 91,* 517-539.

Hirschhorn, L. (1991). *Managing in the new team environment: Skills, tools, and methods.* Reading, MA: Addison-Wesley.

Hirsh, S. K., & Kummerow, J. M. (1990). *Introduction to type in organizations* (2nd ed.). Palo Alto, CA: Consulting Psychologists Press.

Hoffman, L. R. (1959). Homogeneity of member personality and its effect on group problem solving. *Journal of Abnormal and Social Psychology, 58,* 27-32.

Jackson, S. E., & Associates (1992). *Diversity in the workplace: Human resources initiatives.* New York: Guilford Press.

Jackson, S. E., & Alvarez, E. B. (1992). Working through diversity as a strategic impera-tive. In S. E. Jackson (Ed.), *Diversity in the workplace: Human resources initiatives* (pp. 13-29). New York: Guilford Press.

Jackson, S. E., Brett, J. F., Sessa, V. I., Cooper, D. M., Julin, J. A., & Peyronnin, K. (1991). Some differences make a difference: Individual dissimilarity and group heterogeneity as correlates of recruitment, promotions, and turnover. *Journal of Applied Psychology, 76,* 675-689.

Janis, I. L. (1982). *Groupthink: Psychological studies of policy decisions and fiascos.* Boston: Houghton-Mifflin.

Johnston, W. B., & Packer, A. E. (1987). *Workforce 2000: Work and workers for the 21st century.* Indianapolis, IN: Hudson Institute.

Kanter, R. M. (1983). *The change masters.* New York: Simon & Schuster.

Kaplan, R. E. (1979). The conspicuous absence of evidence that process consultation enhances task performance. *Journal of Applied Behavioral Science, 15,* 346-360.

Mandell, B., & Kohler-Gray, S. (1990). Management that values diversity. *Personnel, 67,* 41-47.

Marmer-Solomon, C. (1989, August). The corporate response to workforce diversity. *Personnel Journal,* pp. 43-53.

McCaulley, M. H. (1981). *Jung's theory of psychological types and the Myers-Briggs Type Indicator.* Gainesville, FL: Center for Applications of Psychological Type, Inc.

McGrath, J. E., Berdahl, J. L., & Arrow, H. (1995). Traits, expectations, culture, and clout: The dynamics of diversity in work groups. In S. E. Jackson & M. N. Ruderman (Eds.), *Diversity in work teams: Research paradigms for a changing workplace.* Washington, DC: American Psychological Association.

McLeod, P. L., Lobel, S. A., & Cox, T., Jr. (1993). *Cultural diversity and creativity in small groups: A test of the value in diversity hypothesis.* Unpublished working paper, the University of Michigan at Ann Arbor.

Myers, I. B., & McCaulley, M. H. (1985). *Manual: A guide to the development and use of the Myers-Briggs Type Indicator.* Palo Alto, CA: Consulting Psychologists Press.

Nemeth, C. J. (1986). Differential contributions of majority and minority influence. *Psychological Review, 93,* 23-32.

Ouchi, W. G. (1981). *Theory Z: How American companies can meet the Japanese challenge.* Reading, MA: Addison-Wesley.

Peters, T. J., & Waterman, R. H. (1982). *In search of excellence: Lessons from America's best-run companies.* New York: Harper & Row.

Pritchard, R. A. (1992). Organizational productivity. In M. D. Dunnette (Ed.), *Handbook of industrial/organizational psychology* (2nd ed., Vol. 4). Palo Alto, CA: Consulting Psychologists Press.

Schneider, B. (1987). The people make the place. *Personnel Psychology, 40*(3), 437-453.

Seashore, S. E. (1954). *Group cohesiveness in the industrial work group.* Ann Arbor: University of Michigan Press.

Shea, G. P., & Guzzo, R. A. (1987). Group effectiveness: What really matters? *Sloan Management Review, 28,* 25-31.

Steiner, I. D. (1972). *Group process and productivity.* New York: Free Press.

Sundstrom, E., De Meuse, K., & Futrell, D. (1990). Work teams: Applications and effectiveness. *American Psychologist, 45*(2), 120-133.

Thomas, R. T., Jr. (1991). *Beyond race and gender: Unleashing the power of your total workforce by managing diversity.* New York: AMACOM.

Varney, G. H. (1989). *Building productive teams: An action guide and resource book.* San Francisco: Jossey-Bass.

Willis, C. G. (1985). Myers-Briggs Type Indicator. In D. J. Keyser & R. C. Sweetland (Eds.), *Test critiques* (Vol. 1, pp. 482-490). Kansas City, MO: Westport.

Appendix

FREQUENCY DATA FOR THE DEMOGRAPHIC VARIABLES

Category	Name	Frequency	Percent
Race	Black	15	3.3
	Hispanic	19	4.1
	White	424	92.6
	Missing	18	
Gender	Female	44	9.2
	Male	432	90.8
MBTI	ENFJ	22	6.5
Myers-	ENFP	6	1.8
Briggs	ENTJ	29	8.5
Type	ENTP	9	2.6
Indicator	ESFJ	49	14.4
	ESFP	8	2.3
	ESTJ	119	34.9
	ESTP	14	4.1
	INFJ	4	1.2
	INFP	2	0.6
	INTJ	5	1.5
	INTP	3	0.9
	ISFJ	18	5.3
	ISFP	7	2.1
	ISTJ	39	11.4
	ISTP	7	2.1
	Missing	135	28.4

N = 476.

Author Notes

Differing definitions throughout the literature do not make a clear distinction between effectiveness and productivity as separate constructs; rather, the terms are used somewhat interchangeably. However, it does seem clear that analysis based on either term is context specific. Any research on effectiveness or productivity, and how any variety of factors may affect them, should take into account the context in which they are studied (Gladstein, 1984). Studying groups in context is a difficult task, but as teams become more prevalent in organizations the need for this type of context-specific research becomes more apparent.

Therefore, for the purposes of this study, the term *effectiveness* was defined as the degree to which a team meets the achievable objectives set forth by members of the team and the management of the organization. These objectives included economic measures of team success, attainment of team goals, satisfaction of group members, and the ability of team members to interact effectively. The term *productivity* was defined as a subset of effectiveness based purely on objective economic measures of team performance. The specific criteria used to determine team productivity were presented in the methods section of the paper.

EFFECTS OF GROUP DIVERSITY ON PERCEPTIONS OF GROUP AND SELF AMONG SCIENTISTS AND ENGINEERS

Nancy DiTomaso
Rutgers Faculty of Management

Rene Cordero
The School of Industrial Management
New Jersey Institute of Technology

George F. Farris
Rutgers Faculty of Management

Abstract

This paper examines the effects of work-group heterogeneity, among a sample of scientists and engineers, in terms of three issues: (a) the perceptions of group members of the group process; (b) the perceptions of group members of their own career opportunities; and (c) the sense of well-being of the group members. A survey conducted at 24 U.S.-based industries asked respondents questions about work, career, relations with supervisors and others, work and family, and demographic data. Results suggest that being a minority in the work group creates some psychological discomfort. The effects, however, differ by gender and race/ethnicity.

✳ ✳ ✳

Recent changes in the composition of the labor force have raised many issues about the potential effects of greater heterogeneity in the workplace (Watson, Kumar, & Michaelsen, 1993). Potential effects especially concern those in work settings that have been more homogeneous in the past. Some have argued that heterogeneity will contribute to enhanced creativity and

We would like to acknowledge the support from the Sloan Foundation, Grant No. 93-5-2, and from The Center for Innovation Management Studies, Grant No. LU 427-539. Assistance was also received from the Rutgers University Technology Management Research Center.

productivity of work groups that deal with complex work assignments (Cox & Blake, 1991; Kirchmeyer & McLellan, 1991). The research evidence for such claims, however, is limited (see Lobel & McLeod, 1992). Those who have made these claims have relied on past work on diversity of educational background or perspective (e.g., Hoffman & Maier, 1961; Hoffman, Harburg, & Maier, 1962; Pelz & Andrews, 1976; Triandis, Hall, & Ewen, 1965), not work on ethnicity or gender.

The research evidence, on the contrary, suggests that heterogeneity in small groups expands the potential for misunderstanding, miscommunication, and lack of trust (Steiner, 1972). The reasons for such outcomes are well established. People learn language and symbolic meaning within groups. If one is unaccustomed to interaction with those whose upbringing is different, then there is likely to be miscommunication, even when there is goodwill. That is, there are likely to be problems in communicating effectively with strangers (Gudykunst, 1994; O'Reilly, Caldwell, & Barnett, 1989; Tsui, Egan, & O'Reilly, 1992).

Goodwill, however, cannot always be assumed. To the extent that we categorize ourselves as part of a group (even unconsciously) and make a distinction between ourselves and others, then we also tend to engage in attribution errors (Heider, 1958; Kelley, 1967) regarding the members of the group different from ourselves. We tend to blame them for failure but dismiss their successes, while we take credit for our successes and blame circumstances for our failures (Pettigrew, 1979; Ross, 1977; see discussion in Gudykunst, 1994).

When a group is first formed, it is often the case that there is an initial period of conflict (called *storming*) until the group members establish trust among themselves, a common understanding of the goals for the group, and the rules by which the group will function (called *norming*; Tuchman, 1965). If group members successfully accomplish the norming activity, they can move on to work together effectively. To get to this point, however, may take more effort if the group members begin from different and unspoken assumptions about appropriate ways of thinking and interacting. Thus, extra effort to establish norms in a heterogeneous group may lead to process losses (Jackson, Brett, Sessa, Cooper, Julin, & Peyronnin, 1991). Some have suggested that if a group successfully works through the early difficulties and comes to a common understanding, heterogeneous groups are even more effective than homogeneous groups (Adler, 1986), especially in creative tasks that require the participation of people with different mind-sets. Others have suggested that the likelihood of reaching an effective stage is more problematic for a heterogeneous group, and thus the benefits of diverse backgrounds may be more illusory than real.

Certainly diversity cannot lead to harmonious group interactions unless and until the norming process is established. One of the critical questions regarding diversity in groups, therefore, is whether groups are structured in such a way and are stable enough in membership to get through the "storming" stage and move on to establishing norms. Another, and equally problematic question, is whether group leaders are sufficiently attentive to the need for bridging the differences in a heterogeneous group, such that they are able to facilitate the developmental process that the group needs to work through in order to be effective.

Finally, a question that has been posed but not answered in the literature on work-group diversity is whether the distinctions of gender, race/ethnicity, and nationality are, in themselves, a shorthand code for differences in mind-sets—or backgrounds, frameworks, hidden assumptions, and such (see Katz, Goldston, & Benjamin, 1958). In other words, on what basis would one expect heterogeneity to produce benefits to groups, or conversely, on what basis would one expect process losses because of diversity of gender, race/ethnicity, or nationality?

There is an extensive literature describing differences in cross-cultural values, communication styles, and norms of politeness—enough to fill volumes about the missteps due to violations of norms across cultures (Gudykunst, 1994; Hofstede, 1984, 1993). But are these differences equally salient in interactions among work-group members in the U.S., and do they exist for gender and race/ethnic groups as well? If so, what is it about such groups that causes potential misunderstanding on the one hand or potential richness in points of view on the other?

In this paper we examine the effects of work-group diversity on three types of outcomes: (a) the perceptions of group members of the group process, (b) the perceptions of group members of their own career opportunities in groups with different composition, and (c) the potential effect of work-group composition on the sense of well-being of the group members.

Group Process

A great deal of the literature on group composition focuses on the impact of group composition on the cohesiveness of the group (Ziller, 1973). The research evidence tends to show that homogeneous groups are more cohesive than are heterogeneous groups, and cohesiveness is then positively associated with increased group morale and better communication (Cox,

1993). There is a negative side to group cohesion as well. Too much cohesion can lead to "groupthink," the premature foreclosure of options in decision making (Janis, 1982).

The process of social categorization (Taylor, Fiske, Etcoff, & Ruderman, 1978; Turner, 1987), as already noted, leads to negative attributions of out-group members, which then undermine a sense of trust and commitment. In work settings where subgroup membership is especially salient, therefore, one would expect diverse groups to be less cohesive. The negative effect toward the group can be in either of two directions. Either the majority group can feel more negative toward the group in the presence of minorities; or alternatively, the minority person can feel more negative toward the group because of his or her minority status.

In the work settings we are examining, white males are the majority group (in both numbers and levels of authority). The growing numbers of non-whites in these work settings are primarily Asian males, but they are still in the minority. Women are also a minority among scientists and engineers, and most of the women entering such fields are white. There is a difference, however, between the minority status of non-whites and women among scientists and engineers. Asian scientists and engineers are disproportionately likely to have a Ph.D. compared to white men (National Research Council, 1993; Vetter, 1992a). Women scientists and engineers are less likely to have a Ph.D. than are white men (DiTomaso & Farris, 1994; Vetter, 1992b). The significance of this difference is that having a Ph.D. signifies a level of knowledge that is highly valued in these knowledge-based organizations (Pelz & Andrews, 1976). Thus, an increasing presence of non-whites can also mean the increasing presence of Ph.D.s, while the increasing presence of women can mean the increasing presence of lower-status employees (Noble, 1991; Wharton & Baron, 1987). Thus, we would expect that the reactions to non-whites would be more favorable than the reactions to women in these settings. Furthermore, we would expect women to be more conscious of their subordinate status and thus to be less favorable toward work groups where they are less well represented.

> *Hypothesis 1:* The greater the presence of women in the work group, the more negative we would expect men to be regarding the cohesiveness of the group, the less we would expect men to feel a part of the group, and the lower we would expect men to rate the group's performance. We expect women to react in the opposite way to the greater presence of women in their work groups.

Hypothesis 2: The greater the presence of non-whites in the work group, the more favorable we expect the reactions of non-whites to be in terms of group cohesiveness, feeling a part of the work group, and rating the group's performance. We do not expect the views of whites to vary with the changing proportion of non-whites.

Individual Career Opportunity

The presence of those who are different from oneself in a work group can affect one's own career opportunities in various ways. Being a member of a minority group can cause one to stand out or, alternatively, to be invisible, depending on the dynamics within the group and within the organization (Kanter, 1977a, 1977b; Spangler, Gordon, & Pipkin, 1978). In such a situation one can also be the subject of harassment or of special favor. A minority-group member who sees an advantage to being associated with a more favored majority may actually desire to be in a group with majority-group members. If, however, one expects that one's lower status will be more evident in association with the majority, then one might feel there is greater opportunity in a group of people similar to oneself.

From the opposite point of view, one who is a member of the majority in the organization but a minority in the work group can either hope to gain special privilege by being the only majority-group member in the work group, or can fear guilt by association on the assumption that others will think that those majority-group members who work with lower-status minority-group members may themselves be less worthy of high status.

In terms of career opportunities, these dynamics may differ depending on whether it is conferral of status, reputation, or decision-making authority that one seeks. In an environment in which there is a recognized majority who receives disproportionate favor, one would expect such favor to be extended to most members of the majority, unless they are too closely associated with minority-group members. Thus, one would expect favor to the majority-group members except for those "majority" group members who are in a "minority" (i.e., whites in a group that is majority non-white or men in a group which is majority female). In such situations, these whites or men may feel that their own competence is called into question by being assigned to a group of outsiders. Thus, we would expect:

Hypothesis 3: Because women in research and development (R&D) organizations are a minority, not only in most work groups but also within most (if not all) such organizations, we expect that when men are a minority in the work group that is primarily female, their attitudes regarding career opportunities will be less favorable than when they are a majority in the work group. Specifically, we expect men in a minority position to think others will have less confidence in them, to feel that they have less opportunity to gain recognition in the company, and to feel they have less opportunity to initiate new activities. We expect women who are a minority in the work group to have similarly negative feelings compared to those women who are in the majority in their work groups.

Hypothesis 4: Because whites in R&D organizations are a majority in most work groups and also a majority in such organizations, we would expect those whites who are in a minority in their work groups to expect to receive special treatment. We expect non-whites in these work settings to be less favorable about being in groups that are majority non-white than about being in groups that are majority white. Specifically, we expect non-whites to feel others will have more confidence in them, that they will have more opportunity to gain recognition in the company, and that they will have greater opportunity to initiate new activities in groups that are majority white. We expect whites either to expect no difference in treatment or to perceive even more career opportunities when they are in groups that are majority non-white.

Diversity and a Sense of Well-being

For the same reasons that we expect women and non-whites to be more favorable about group processes when in groups with similar others, we also expect them to feel more comfortable when there are more people in the group like themselves. Because of the potential negative attributions that may be directed toward them in groups in which they are a minority, we would expect women and non-whites to feel they could get a fairer evaluation in a group with similar others. We also expect that they will enjoy their work more and will perceive less stress when they are not in a minority position. Thus,

Hypothesis 5: We expect that women will be less likely to feel they can get a fair evaluation, less likely to say they enjoy their work, and less likely to say their jobs involve low stress (i.e., more likely to experience stress) in jobs with fewer women.

Hypothesis 6: We expect that non-whites will be less likely to feel that they can get a fair evaluation, less likely to say they enjoy their work, and less likely to say their jobs involve low stress (i.e., more likely to experience stress) in jobs with fewer non-whites.

Method

The data used in these analyses were taken from a survey conducted by the authors from 1990 to 1992 at 24 U.S.-based industrial companies. The survey instrument was developed by the authors, using questions from previous studies of scientists and engineers (e.g., Pelz & Andrews, 1976), as well as questions developed by the authors from focus groups and interviews conducted at 5 companies with about 100 scientists and engineers prior to the survey (DiTomaso, Farris, & Cordero, 1993). The survey included questions on work, career, relations with supervisors and others, work and family, and demographic data. Only some of the data from the survey were used in these analyses. There were 3,163 respondents to the survey, and the overall response rate for the survey was 55% (although only 6 organizations fell below this level). The average response rate across the other 18 companies was 65%.

Dependent Variables

In this paper, we use three types of dependent variables: evaluations by the respondent of the group process, evaluations by the respondent of his or her own career opportunities, and evaluations by the respondent of his or her sense of well-being. In all cases, we have information only from individuals reporting about the characteristics of their work groups or their perceptions of the work situations. Although such individual-level data may not provide a direct test of the effects of group composition on the outcomes for the group members, this type of analysis does provide an estimate of how the perceptions group members have are influenced by the amount of diversity present.

Group process. We measured three aspects of group process: the respondent's perception of the cohesion of the group, the extent to which the respondent feels a part of the group, and the evaluation by the respondent of the group's performance. The group-cohesion measure was created based on factor analysis results (using a maximum likelihood procedure; all scaled from 1 [not at all] to 7 [very great]) for a set of questions that assessed the extent to which: (a) the group members have confidence and trust in one another, (b) the group members support one another, (c) the group members are familiar with one another's tasks, (d) the group members are enthusiastic, (e) the group is more creative than the individual members, (f) the group builds on each other's ideas, (g) all group members can influence the direction of the group, and (h) the group members have a lot of difference of opinion before decisions are made. (The factor analysis yielded one factor, which explained 57% of the variance.) Feeling part of the group is a single item measuring the respondent's answer to a question about the extent to which he or she feels "really a part of the group" (on a scale from 1 [not at all] to 7 [very great]). The rating of the group's performance is also a single item on which the respondent was asked to rate his or her own group's performance "compared to other similar groups" (on a scale from 1 [much worse than others] to 7 [much better than others]).

Career opportunities. Individual career opportunities also were assessed using three measures: An assessment of how much confidence the respondent believes others have in him or her, the extent to which the respondent feels that he or she has the opportunity to build his or her reputation in the company, and the extent to which the respondent has the opportunity to initiate new activities or invent new products and processes. Confidence of others was measured with a single item worded as follows, "Consider four or five people in your organization whose opinion of you matters most to you. In general, how much confidence do you believe they have in your abilities?" The scaling ranged from 1 (no confidence) to 7 (complete confidence). Recognition in the company was measured by a single item indicating the extent to which the respondent felt his or her job provided the opportunity to "build my professional reputation within this company" (scored 1 [slight or none] to 7 [utmost]). Opportunity to initiate new activities was measured by use of factor analysis (again, using a maximum likelihood procedure) of the extent to which the job provides an opportunity to "have responsibility for initiating new activities," "help technical personnel grow and develop," and "invent new products or processes." The factor analysis yielded a single factor (which explained 50% of the variance).

Well-being. Sense of well-being was measured in three ways: An evaluation by the respondent regarding the opportunity to be evaluated fairly, the extent to which the respondent indicated that he or she enjoyed work, and an indicator that the job provided low stress. Fairness of evaluation was measured with a single item regarding the opportunity the respondent has on the job "to be evaluated fairly in proportion to what I contribute" (score from 1 [slight or none] to 7 [utmost]). Enjoying work was measured with a single item regarding the extent to which the respondent felt that his or her job provides the opportunity "to enjoy my work and look forward to each day" (scored from 1 [slight or none] to 7 [utmost]). Finally, low stress was measured using items that were identified by a principal components analysis (eigenvalue of 1.49). These two items assessed the extent to which the respondent's job provides the opportunity to "have sufficient time left for my personal or family life" and "having a job that is not stressful" (scored from 1 [slight or none] to 7 [utmost]).

Independent Variables

We created dummy variables for both gender and race/ethnicity to provide an assessment of the respondent's demographic group in relationship to the composition of the work group (formed by multiplying the dummy variables for either gender or race/ethnicity by the proportion of women or non-whites in the work group). To create these dummy variables, we first constructed a measure of work-group composition in terms of proportion female or proportion non-white (both ranging from 0 to 1.00). The average proportion of women across the groups was .24 and the average proportion of non-whites was .22. Because it would be difficult to see how the change in the proportion affected the perceptions of group members by using the distribution itself, we created dummy variables for different proportions of gender or race/ethnic diversity. We divided the distributions across all groups into four categories: groups with less than 10% females (or non-white), groups with 11 to 30% females (or non-white), groups with 31 to 50% females (or non-white), and groups with more than 50% females (or non-white).

We then created 8 dummy variables for gender, each of which was coded 1 (if in the group) or 0: men in groups with 10% or fewer females (MaleProp1), men in groups with 11 to 30% females (MaleProp2), men in groups with 31 to 50% females (MaleProp3), men in groups with more than 50% females (MaleProp4), women in groups with 10% or fewer females (FemaleProp1), females in groups with 11 to 30% females (FemaleProp2), females in groups with 31 to 50% females (FemaleProp3), and females in groups with more than 50% females (FemaleProp4). Eight dummy variables were similarly created for variations in the race/ethnic composition of the groups (for example, whites in groups with 10% or fewer non-whites, and so on; WhtProp1, WhtProp2, WhtProp3, WhtProp4, NwhtProp1, NwhtProp2, NwhtProp3, NwhtProp4). Tables 1 and 2 provide the breakdown of the groups reported by the respondents. In analyses of both gender and race/

ethnicity, we use as the reference category male (or whites) in groups with less than 10% females (or non-whites).

Table 1. Gender Distribution by Proportion Female in Work Groups*

Gender	Proportion			
	<.10	.11 – .30	.31 – .50	>.50
Men	782 (34%)	962 (41%)	465 (20%)	113 (5%)
Women	29 (4%)	240 (35%)	271 (40%)	138 (20%)

*Numbers may not add up to 100 because of rounding error.

Table 2. Race Distribution by Proportion Non-white in Work Groups*

Race	Proportion			
	<.10	.11 – .30	.31 – .50	>.50
White	672 (28%)	983 (41%)	567 (24%)	193 (8%)
Non-white	135 (23%)	215 (37%)	171 (30%)	59 (10%)

*Numbers may not add up to 100 because of rounding error.

We ran separate regression analyses (Ordinary Least Squares Regression) of each dependent variable by gender and by race/ethnicity. Thus, the analyses test the effects either of the proportion of females in the group or of the proportion of non-whites (but not both simultaneously). In all equations we also included a control for Ph.D. (1 = Ph.D. degree, 0 = no Ph.D. degree) and the age of the respondent (in years). These were included because, as noted, women are less likely to have Ph.D.s and non-whites are more likely to have them. Women and non-whites were also both younger, on average, than were men and whites in this sample. Finally, we included a control for the size of the group (adding together the number of men and number of women reported by the respondent) and for the age of the group, from a single item, asking the respondent the extent to which the group "has been working together a long time" (scored from 1 [not at all] to 7 [very great]). There were 3,163 valid surveys returned in the study. The actual N for these equations varies because of missing data on one or more of the variables. Tables 3a and 3b provide the means, standard deviations, and correlations for the variables used in the analysis.

Table 3a. Means, Standard Deviations, and Correlations

Variable	*N*	*M*	*SD*
MaleProp1	3022	.26	.44
MaleProp2	3022	.32	.47
MaleProp3	3022	.15	.36
MaleProp4	3022	.04	.19
FemaleProp1	3022	.01	.10
FemaleProp2	3022	.08	.27
FemaleProp3	3022	.09	.29
FemaleProp4	3022	.05	.21
WhtProp1	3022	.33	.47
WhtProp2	3022	.28	.45
WhtProp3	3022	.14	.35
WhtProp4	3022	.04	.20
NwhtProp1	3022	.01	.09
NwhtProp2	3022	.06	.25
NwhtProp3	3022	.07	.25
NwhtProp4	3022	.05	.22
Group Cohesion	2949	.00	.96
Feel Part of Group	3006	4.94	1.52
Rating of Group	2980	4.95	1.22
Confidence of Others	3019	5.49	1.03
Recognition in Company	3007	3.95	1.39
Opportunity to Initiate	2952	.00	.90
Fair Evaluation	2999	3.99	1.46
Enjoy Work	3004	4.26	1.51
Low Stress	2989	.00	1.00
Group Size	3022	9.04	4.17
Group Age	3002	3.49	1.58

Table 3b. Correlations of Proportion Variables with Dependent Variables

Group Proportions	Dependent Variables								
	Group Cohesion	Feel Part of Group	Rating of Group	Confidence of Others	Recognition in Company	Opportunity to Initiate	Fair Evaluation	Enjoy Work	Low Stress
Male Proportion 1	.08***	.05*	.03+	.01	.04*	.02	.01	.04*	.07***
Male Proportion 2	.03	.02	.00	.04*	-.01	.02	-.01	.01	.01
Male Proportion 3	-.02	.00	-.01	.02	.02	.03	.00	.01	-.03
Male Proportion 4	-.04*	.01	.01	-.02	.02	.02	-.00	.01	-.01
Female Proportion 1	-.05*	-.05**	-.01	-.03+	-.03+	-.04+	.00	-.04+	-.04+
Female Proportion 2	-.06**	-.04**	-.04*	-.04*	-.03+	-.04*	-.02	-.03	-.04*
Female Proportion 3	-.02	-.02	-.04*	-.03+	-.05**	-.06**	.01	-.04*	-.01
Female Proportion 4	-.01	.00	.02	.00	.03	.00	.04	-.02	-.03
White Proportion 1	.03	.01	.03	.00	-.04*	-.03	.02	.00	.05
White Proportion 2	.01	-.00	-.02	.01	.04*	.06**	.05**	.03+	.01
White Proportion 3	-.01	-.00	-.01	.04*	.02	.01	.01	.02	-.01
White Proportion 4	-.06**	.00	-.03+	.02	-.01	-.01	-.05*	-.03	-.03+
Non-white Proportion 1	.01	.99	.00	.02	.03+	.02	.02	.02	.04*
Non-white Proportion 2	.01	-.01	.01	-.02	-.01	-.03+	-.01	-.02	.01
Non-white Proportion 3	-.02	-.01	-.00	-.05**	.01	.00	-.04*	-.02	-.04*
Non-white Proportion 4	.01	.01	.02	-.05**	-.04	-.04*	-.04*	-.03+	-.07***

*** $p < .001$; ** $p < .01$; * $p < .05$; + $p < .10$

Results

Tables 4a and 4b provide the results of the analyses for the respondents' perceptions of group process. As expected by *Hypothesis 1* (see p. 102), women were less likely to perceive group cohesion in groups that were more than 70% male, but their perceptions were not much different from men in groups with at least 30% women (the coefficients are negative but not statistically significant at conventional levels). Men were negative about group cohesion in those groups that were majority female. The same pattern is evident in the responses regarding feeling a part of the group. Women were less likely to feel included in groups with fewer than 30% female, while men were less likely to feel included in groups that were majority female. We did not, however, find this pattern in the evaluation of the group's performance. Women in groups that were 30 to 50% female rated their groups lower than did men in groups that were mostly male, but this effect was only marginally significant. In addition, we found that the larger the group, the less cohesive it was perceived to be on all three dependent variables, and the longer the group had been together, the more cohesive it was perceived to be.

Table 4a. Gender Diversity and Group Process
(Unstandardized Regression Coefficients)

	Dependent Variables		
Independent Variables	**Group Cohesion**	**Feel Part of Group**	**Rating of Group**
Ph.D.	–.02	–.00	.04
Age of Employee	.00	.00	.01*
MaleProp2	–.03	.02	–.05
MaleProp3	–.08	.01	–.03
MaleProp4	–.26**	–.32*	–.01
FemaleProp1	–.47*	–.74**	–.04
FemaleProp2	–.24***	–.27*	–.14
FemaleProp3	–.10	–.12	–.16+
FemaleProp4	–.14+	–.04	.12
Size of Group	–.03***	–.04***	–.01*
Age of Group	.16***	.19***	.20***
Adjusted R^2	.09	.05	.07
N	2875	2909	2885

*** $p < .001$; ** $p < .01$; * $p < .05$; + $p < .10$

Table 4b. Race/Ethnicity Diversity and Group Process
(Unstandardized Regression Coefficients)

Independent Variables	Dependent Variables		
	Group Cohesion	Feel Part of Group	Rating of Group
Ph.D.	−.00	.01	.04
Age of Employee	.00	.00	.01**
WhtProp2	−.04	.05	−.04
WhtProp3	−.00	.06	−.04
WhtProp4	−.25**	.09	−.26*
NwhtProp1	.13	.15	.09
NwhtProp2	.00	−.00	−.02
NwhtProp3	−.04	.02	.00
NwhtProp4	−.03	.01	.04
Size of Group	−.03***	−.04***	−.02**
Age of Group	.16***	.20***	.20***
Adjusted R^2	.08	.05	.07
N	2875	2909	2885

*** $p < .001$; ** $p < .01$; * $p < .05$

The same pattern was not evident for the analyses by race/ethnicity, contrary to what we expected under *Hypothesis 2* (see p. 103). For non-whites, we found no significant relationships between the three measures of group composition and group process. The only significant effect was that whites in groups that were majority non-white indicated less cohesiveness than whites in groups that were mostly white. We found the same pattern for the rating of the group's performance. We found no significant effects regarding feeling a part of the group. Again, we found significant negative effects with the size of the group and significant positive effects for the length of time the group had been together.

Tables 5a and 5b show the results of the analyses for the three measures of individual career opportunity. *Hypothesis 3* (see p. 103) was supported by the responses of women, but it was not supported by the responses of men. Women were less likely to feel they had opportunities in groups that were majority male, but there was no relationship between the composition of the group and men's evaluation of their career opportunities. The pattern of coefficients for women were consistent in the prediction of the confidence of others, although most of the coefficients just missed statistical significance. Women were more negative about their opportunity to build their reputations

Table 5a. Gender Diversity and Individual Opportunity
(Unstandardized Regression Coefficients)

	Dependent Variables		
Independent Variables	**Confidence of Others**	**Recognition in Company**	**Opportunity to Initiate**
Ph.D.	.04	.17**	.20***
Age of Employee	.00[+]	−.01*	.00
MaleProp2	.05	−.11	−.01
MaleProp3	.02	.04	.03
MaleProp4	−.14	.08	.06
FemaleProp1	−.31	−.60*	−.36*
FemaleProp2	−.14[+]	−.26*	−.11[+]
FemaleProp3	−.12	−.35***	−.16*
FemaleProp4	.03	.14	.06
Size of Group	.01	.01*	.01[+]
Age of Group	.06***	.06***	.07***
Adjusted R^2	.01	.01	.03
N	2921	2909	2865

*** $p < .001$; ** $p < .01$; * $p < .05$; [+] $p < .10$

Table 5b. Race/Ethnicity Diversity and Individual Opportunity
(Unstandardized Regression Coefficients)

	Dependent Variables		
Independent Variables	**Confidence of Others**	**Recognition in Company**	**Opportunity to Initiate**
Ph.D.	.06	.19***	.21***
Age of Employee	.00*	−.00	.00[+]
WhtProp2	.01	.13[+]	.11*
WhtProp3	.10	.10	.03
WhtProp4	.06	−.04	−.02
NwhtProp1	.28	.53*	.29[+]
NwhtProp2	−.06	.01	−.11
NwhtProp3	−.18*	.06	.06
NwhtProp4	−.20*	−.25*	−.15[+]
Size of Group	.00	.01	.00
Age of Group	.06***	.06***	.07***
Adjusted R^2	.02	.01	.04
N	2921	2909	2865

*** $p < .001$; ** $p < .01$; * $p < .05$; [+] $p < .10$

in the company and about their opportunities to initiate new activities when they were in the minority. Only in groups that were majority female did women not differ from men on these measures.

Once again we found that the pattern for non-whites was not consistent with that of women. Non-whites were less likely to feel they had opportunities in groups that were more than 30% non-white. Whites were more likely to feel that they had the opportunity to gain recognition and to initiate new activities in groups that were mostly white, and non-whites also felt they had more opportunity when they worked alongside whites. Thus, it appears that whites received preferred treatment in all groups. Being together a longer time enhanced the respondent's sense of opportunity, and in this case, the size of the group did not detract from opportunity.

Tables 6a and 6b provide the results of the analyses regarding the sense of well-being. In this case, we found mixed results. Employees did not seem to differ in their assessment of whether they were being evaluated fairly. The coefficients for women went from negative to positive with the shift in the composition, but they were not statistically significant. Women were less likely in male-dominated groups, however, to say they enjoyed their work. Women reported more stress in all groups compared to men in groups which

Table 6a. Gender Diversity and Sense of Well-being
(Unstandardized Regression Coefficients)

Independent Variables	Dependent Variables		
	Fair Evaluation	**Enjoy Work**	**Low Stress**
Ph.D.	.08	.07	.00
Age of Employee	−.02***	.00	−.00
MaleProp2	−.03	−.07	−.08
MaleProp3	−.03	−.07	−.14*
MaleProp4	−.01	−.03	−.13
FemaleProp1	−.15	−.62*	−.46*
FemaleProp2	−.21+	−.22+	−.25**
FemaleProp3	−.05	−.29*	−.14+
FemaleProp4	.19	−.15	−.25*
Size of Group	.01	.01	−.01+
Age of Group	.09***	.08***	.03*
Adjusted R^2	.02	.01	.01
N	2902	2906	2923

*** $p < .001$; ** $p < .01$; * $p < .05$; + $p < .10$

Table 6b. Race/Ethnicity Diversity and Sense of Well-being
(Unstandardized Regression Coefficients)

	Dependent Variables		
Independent Variables	**Fair Evaluation**	**Enjoy Work**	**Low Stress**
Ph.D.	.09	.10	.04
Age of Employee	−.02***	.00	−.00
WhtProp2	.05	.06	−.04
WhtProp3	−.02	.05	−.08
WhtProp4	−.42**	−.23	−.22*
NwhtProp1	.18	.28	.36[+]
NwhtProp2	−.17	−.15	−.06
NwhtProp3	−.29*	−.11	−.21**
NwhtProp4	−.42**	−.27*	−.41***
Size of Group	.00	.00	−.02
Age of Group	.10***	.09	.03*
Adjusted R^2	.02	.01	.01*
N	2902	2906	2923

*** $p < .001$; ** $p < .01$; * $p < .05$; [+] $p < .10$

had less than 10% women, but the greatest effects for women were in those groups with the fewest women.

Contrary to expectation, non-whites were least likely to feel they can get a fair evaluation or to enjoy their work in groups with more than 30% non-whites, and whites similarly were more negative about groups which were majority non-white, namely, that they were less likely to be evaluated fairly or to enjoy work. Low stress, however, was more evident for both non-whites and whites in groups that were a majority non-white.

Discussion and Conclusions

These analyses should be considered tentative, in that the individual-level data cannot directly test the effects of group processes. In all cases, we find that although the effects are statistically significant, they do not account for much explained variation in the dependent variables. Further, the results differ for women and for non-whites. The lower status of women in these types of organizations seems to create a situation in which women are at a disadvantage when there are few other women in their groups. They perceive less cohesion and feel less a part of the group. They perceive less opportunity to get ahead, and they are more negative about their experiences. They do not, as a consequence, however, consistently rate the group performance lower. Non-whites, in contrast, appear to be more favorable about their work situation when they are in groups that are majority white. Apparently, given their higher educational status, on average, they want to associate primarily with the majority and do not want to become part of a ghettoized minority in these work situations. In majority non-white groups, non-whites evidently feel they lose status and also a sense of well-being.

The analyses in this paper suggest a number of important conclusions, however tentative. First, it appears that we need to look at both sides of the potential interactions among majority- and minority-group members. We cannot automatically assume negative attributions will be evident because of the individual or group-level interaction. We must, in addition, consider the context. In this case, the stronger position of non-whites compared to women evidently moderates the reactions which we might otherwise expect from non-whites to being a part of a minority group. Second, the evidence here of some psychological discomfort at being in a lower-status or minority position, even in the case of women, does not necessarily translate to more negative evaluations of performance. Finally, in these analyses we tried to determine the possible effects of work-group composition on the responses to our survey. Most notable in this regard is that the effects are so modest. On a number of analyses in which we might have expected some effect, we found none (e.g., opportunity for advancement or professional recognition). In other analyses, we found effects that suggested simple gender or race/ethnic effects, but not an interaction between these and work-group composition.

What do these results mean in terms of the original question regarding the effects of diversity on work-group performance? We find almost no direct effect on performance. We find some evidence for psychological discomfort of those in the minority, but this appears to be mediated by other aspects of the relationship (e.g., also being male, having advanced education, the contextual situation in which the work group finds itself). We expect that whatever effects are evident that they are more problematic in groups which have not developed norms for working together effectively, but we could not demonstrate that in these data without making the analyses even more complicated. Clearly the size of the group and the length of time the group has been together are the major determinants of how individuals feel about the group and how the group works together. Whether the faster pace of work in which groups come together and dissipate without much sustained interaction may exacerbate whatever marginal effects may exist is a question still to be answered. Further, despite the modest effects, the patterns appear consistent, and thus, this may be a case in which small effects accumulate and play a role in such outcomes as satisfaction, turnover, and creativity.

Future research needs to be attentive to the details of interaction and how employees respond to being different. We cannot assume that all such processes work the same way for all groups and that all differences are consequential. We do not know from these analyses whether the kinds of outcomes which seem evident are primarily the result of the interaction among the group members themselves or whether the manager or group leader can intervene to facilitate the group's working together more effectively. Certainly the topic of how the leader responds to and with groups of different types and composition is a major subject of concern that could benefit from subsequent research and study.

References

Adler, N. J. (1986). *International dimensions of organizational behavior.* Boston: Kent Publishing Co.

Cox, T., Jr. (1993). *Cultural diversity in organizations: Theory, research, and practice.* San Francisco: Berrett-Koehler.

Cox, T. H., & Blake, S. (1991). Managing cultural diversity: Implications for organizational competitiveness. *Academy of Management Executive, 5,* 45-56.

DiTomaso, N., & Farris, G. F. (1994, April). Degrees and diversity at work. *IEEE Spectrum,* pp. 38-42.

DiTomaso, N., Farris, G. F., & Cordero, R. (1993). Diversity in the technical workforce: Rethinking the management of scientists and engineers. *Journal of Engineering and Technology Management, 10,* 101-127.

Gudykunst, W. B. (1994). *Bridging differences: Effective intergroup communication* (2nd ed.). Thousand Oaks, CA: Sage.

Heider, F. (1958). *The psychology of interpersonal relations.* New York: John Wiley.

Hoffman, L. R., Harburg, E., & Maier, N. R. F. (1962). Differences and disagreement as factors in creative group problem solving. *Journal of Abnormal and Social Psychology, 64,* 206-214.

Hoffman, L. R., & Maier, N. R. F. (1961). Quality and acceptance of problem solutions by members of homogeneous and heterogeneous groups. *Journal of Abnormal and Social Psychology, 62,* 401-407.

Hofstede, G. (1984). *Culture's consequences: International differences in work-related values.* Beverly Hills, CA: Sage.

Hofstede, G. (1993). Cultural constraints in management theories. *The Executive, 7*(1), 81-94.

Jackson, S. E., Brett, J. F., Sessa, V. I., Cooper, D. M., Julin, J. A., & Peyronnin, K. (1991). Some differences make a difference: Individual dissimilarity and group heterogeneity as correlates of recruitment, promotions, and turnover. *Journal of Applied Psychology, 75*(5), 675-689.

Janis, I. (1982). *Groupthink* (2nd ed.). Boston: Houghton-Mifflin.

Kanter, R. M. (1977a). *Men and women of the corporation.* New York: Basic Books.

Kanter, R. M. (1977b). Some effects of proportions on group life: Skewed sex ratios and responses to token women. *American Journal of Sociology, 82,* 965-990.

Katz, I., Goldston, J., & Benjamin, L. (1958). Behavior and productivity in bi-racial work groups. *Human Relations, 11,* 123-141.

Kelley, H. H. (1967). Attribution theory in social psychology. *Nebraska Symposium on Motivation, 15,* 192-238.

Kirchmeyer, C., & McLellan, J. (1991). Capitalizing on ethnic diversity: An approach to managing the diversity workgroups of the 1990s. *RCSA/Canadian Journal of Administrative Sciences, 8*(2), 72-79.

Lobel, S. A., & McLeod, P. L. (1992). The effects of ethnic diversity on idea generation in small groups. *Proceedings of the Academy of Management Meetings.*

National Research Council (1993). *Summary report 1992: Doctoral recipients from United States universities.* Washington, DC: National Academy Press.

Noble, D. F. (1991). A world without women. *Technology Review, 95,* 52-60.

O'Reilly, C. A., III, Caldwell, D. F., & Barnett, W. P. (1989). Work group demography, social integration, and turnover. *Administrative Science Quarterly, 34,* 21-37.

Pelz, D. C., & Andrews, F. M. (1976). *Scientists in organizations: Productive climates for research and development.* Ann Arbor, MI: Institute for Social Research.

Pettigrew, T. F. (1979). The ultimate attribution error. *Personality and Social Psychology Bulletin, 5,* 461-476.

Ross, L. (1977). The intuitive psychologist and his shortcomings. *Advances in Experimental Psychology and Social Psychology, 10,* 174-220.

Spangler, E., Gordon, M. A., & Pipkin, R. M. (1978). Token women: An empirical test of Kanter's hypothesis. *American Journal of Sociology, 84*(1), 160-170.

Steiner, I. D. (1972). *Group process and productivity.* San Diego, CA: Academic Press.

Taylor, S. E., Fiske, S. T., Etcoff, N. L., & Ruderman, A. J. (1978). Categorical and contextual bases of person memory and stereotyping. *Journal of Personality and Social Psychology, 36,* 718-793.

Triandis, H. C., Hall, E. R., & Ewen, R. B. (1965). Member heterogeneity and dyadic creativity. *Human Relations, 18,* 33-35.

Tsui, A. S., Egan, T. D., & O'Reilly, C. A., III (1992). Being different: Relational demography and organizational attachment. *Administrative Science Quarterly, 37,* 549-579.

Tuchman, B. W. (1965). Developmental sequences in small groups. *Psychological Bulletin, 63,* 384-399.

Turner, J. C. (1987). *Rediscovering the social group: A self-categorization theory.* New York: Basil Blackwell.

Vetter, B. M. (1992a). *Foreign citizens among U.S. scientists and engineers.* Washington, DC: Commission on Professionals in Science and Technology, Occasional Paper 92-2, August.

Vetter, B. M. (1992b). *What's holding up the glass ceiling? Barriers to women in the science and engineering workforce.* Washington, DC: Commission on Professionals in Science and Technology, Occasional Paper 92-3, November.

Watson, W. E., Kumar, K., & Michaelsen, L. K. (1993). Cultural diversity's impact on interaction process and performance: Comparing homogeneous and diverse task groups. *Academy of Management Journal, 36*(3), 590-602.

Wharton, A. S., & Baron, J. N. (1987). So happy together? The impact of gender segregation on men at work. *American Sociological Review, 52,* 574-587.

Ziller, R. C. (1973). Homogeneity and heterogeneity of group members. In C. H. McClintock (Ed.), *Experimental social psychology* (pp. 385-411). New York: Holt, Rinehart & Winston.

THE LIMITATIONS OF ORGANIZATIONAL DEMOGRAPHY: CAN DIVERSITY CLIMATE BE ENHANCED IN THE ABSENCE OF TEAMWORK?

Ellen Ernst Kossek
School of Labor and Industrial Relations
Michigan State University

Susan C. Zonia
College of Osteopathic Medicine
Michigan State University

Willard Young
Ford Motor Company

Abstract

This paper examines the efficacy of one of the most common diversity practices, diversity enlargement. Diversity enlargement *refers to attempts to increase the representations of individuals of different gender, ethnic, and cultural backgrounds in an organization. It is based on psychological theories of social contact, which suggest that increasing the level of contact between members of different identity groups will lead to a reduction in prejudice and stereotyping. Organizations using diversity-enlargement strategies implicitly assume that the climate for diversity (i.e., attitudes about and support for diversity) will be improved through increased contact between members of different social-identity groups.*

The analysis of survey and records data from employees at a large university demonstrated that increasing racial and gender diversity over an eight-year period does not unconditionally result in a more favorable climate for diversity. Diversity enlargement is a necessary but insufficient strategy to enhance diversity climate. The authors identify some dimensions of the climate for diversity that may be improved by diversity-enlargement initiatives. They also point out that organizations have been unclear about what goals they hope to achieve as a result of diversity enlargement. This paper suggests that to enhance diversity climate, diversity-enlargement initiatives must be coupled with interventions in group process.

✷ ✷ ✷

In recent years, many employing organizations have made it a priority to mirror the social and demographic environments in which they function by increasing the representation of individuals of different gender, ethnic, and cultural backgrounds in their firms. We label this strategy *diversity enlargement*. Its implicit assumption is that increasing the diversity of a workforce will over time shift the organizational climate to be more supportive of multiculturalism, ultimately changing an organization's demographic composition, increasing its employees' exposure to people of color (Morrison, 1992), and reducing the phenomenon of tokenism (Kanter, 1977).

Diversity-enlargement strategies are essentially grounded in assumptions from psychology, namely the social contact theory (Allport, 1954): The greater the level of contact and familiarity with members of different social-identity groups, the greater the attraction and the lower the tendency to engage in negative stereotyping. Despite the general widespread nature of this approach, no empirical studies have been published that demonstrate that increasing diversity over time is a sufficient strategy to enhance diversity climate.

Diversity climate refers to the influence of the organizational context on employee attitudes and behaviors that respond to those perceptions of phenomena construed as relevant to diversity (Kossek & Zonia, 1993). *Diversity* pertains to the extent of differences found within a group of people. These differences reflect any attribute that group members use to inform themselves that other members are different from themselves (Triandis, Kurowski, & Gelfand, 1994). Our focus on employee perceptions builds on Schneider and Reichers' (1983) general work on organizational climate: The assumption is that organizations can have a number of climates, each with a referent that provides meaning to psychological clusters of events.[†]

In this article, the referent is diversity climate, which centers on perceptions related to the direct and indirect influence of intergroup dynamics and organizational demography involving race, ethnicity, or gender. Although

---

[†] The term "diversity climate" has been used in a different way by Cox (1993) in his book, *Cultural Diversity in Organizations: Theory, Research, and Practice*. He defines climate more broadly to include a set of individual factors (personal identity structures, prejudice, stereotyping, and personality type), three intergroup factors (cultural differences, ethnocentrism, and intergroup conflict), and four organizational context factors (organizational culture and acculturation processes, structural integration, informal integration, and institutional bias). Our work is consistent with Cox's in that we argue that members' individual attitudes reflect the influence of group and organizational factors that create the context for individual perceptions of intergroup dynamics and the perceived state of organizational multiculturalism.

other kinds of diversity such as age, sexuality, disability, socioeconomic status, and functional orientation are becoming increasingly salient workforce distinctions, we believe that employer efforts to promote multiculturalism have had the greatest psychological link to issues of race, ethnicity, and gender. This is because diversity programs can be historically and conceptually associated with affirmative action efforts since they both share an emphasis on increasing the organizational integration of individuals who differ from white American men (Kossek & Zonia, 1994).

Most of the studies on diversity have used cross-sectional data (see, for example, Kossek & Zonia, 1993). The problem with cross-sectional data is that since attitudes change slowly, in order for the diversity climate to reflect change, members must have had an opportunity to experience interacting with a diversity of individuals before measurable changes in attitudes will be observed. Another problem is that little research has delineated the specific affective changes that should occur if human resource strategies are successfully implemented.

Research Questions and Study Hypotheses

In considering the limitations of previous research and in an effort to fill the gaps described above, the following research questions were addressed:

To what extent does increasing racial and gender diversity over time (in work groups and in organizational units) relate to the climate for diversity? Although some research has found that exposure to professionals who have a different background from one's own can increase breadth and openness (Morrison, 1992), other research shows that the amount of contact with people of color on the job has little impact on racist attitudes of white men (Fernandez, 1991). To date, there has been no evidence that such strategies by themselves will necessarily be related to a favorable diversity climate. We contend that much of the current research and practice focused on workplace diversity has overemphasized changing organizational demography through diversity enlargement. In order to enhance the climate for diversity, we believe the organization must also change the design of human resource and organizational systems to be supportive of engaging in intergroup teamwork.

What are some of the dimensions that might comprise the climate for diversity? Although some work has been done (e.g., Cox, 1993; Kossek & Zonia, 1993), generally, the literature lacks measures that specifically assess diversity climate.

To what extent is variation in attitudes regarding diversity climate a function of individual demographic differences versus changes in organizational demography over time? Kossek and Zonia (1993) have shown, using cross-sectional data, that variation in attitudes toward an employer's effort to enhance diversity was explained more by individual background demographics than by the current racial or gender heterogeneity of one's work group. No studies have been published examining how changes in the organization's demography over time relate to diversity climate, which is an important issue given the pervasiveness of diversity enlargement as a change strategy in U.S. corporations. The degree to which one is dissimilar to other group members relates to variance in attitudes regarding diversity climate and has not been explored. This fact is important because proportional representation is likely to relate to the level of tokenism and stereotyping.

This study asked the overall question of whether diversity-enlargement programs in organizations succeed in fostering more familiarity with diverse groups. The specific hypotheses were:

Hypothesis 1: Increasing the racial and gender heterogeneity of an organizational unit over time will positively relate to diversity climate.

Hypothesis 2: Assuming diversity-enlargement activities have been successfully implemented, contextual variables of work-group and organizational demography will be strongly related to diversity climate, as well as to differences in personal social identities.

These hypotheses were tested in an exploratory study at nineteen colleges in a large public university. Although the study was conducted in an academic setting, the questions asked in the survey and the outcomes derived from them pertain to a broader organizational audience.

In the following sections, we discuss the characteristics of a viable diversity climate and then examine the variables used to investigate the above hypotheses.

Dimensions of Diversity Climate Present, Assuming Diversity-enlargement Programs Are Successful

Our knowledge is limited regarding the ways in which an organization's climate for diversity might be enhanced by implementing diversity-enlargement approaches. This study presents some exploratory dimensions (see Table 1) of diversity climate that are grounded in previous research. These dimensions were suggested by the following reasoning: Assuming one believes that hiring people with diverse backgrounds improves the climate for diversity, members would hold general perceptions reflecting favorable affect, cognitions, and behaviors supporting the value of organizational efforts related to diversity enlargement. Additionally, members would perceive the organization to be sensitive to the issues of multiculturalism and at the same time would be fair in the equal treatment of individuals.

The dimensions in Table 1 range from the holding of general positive affect, beliefs, and behavioral self-reports regarding the change effort (e.g., diversity enlargement enhances organizational effectiveness and top management is committed to the change) to specific measures of a positive diversity climate (e.g., multicultural issues are regularly considered, one's work group has a good mix of backgrounds, and people are fairly treated regardless of their cultural or gender backgrounds). If diversity-enlargement techniques are successful, the characteristics of diversity climate outlined in Table 1 should appear. These outcomes include: members would highly value employer efforts to manage diversity; they would believe senior management is committed; that minorities and women are qualified; that individual rights are protected and respected; that their work group has a good mix; that there is a high level of voluntary interaction with individuals of different backgrounds; and that efforts are made to promote the contributions of all members.

Theoretical Rationale for Selection of Independent Variables

Although we will be unable to infer causality from our data, it may show the existence of a relationship between changes in organizational demography and perceived climate. We believed that three classes of variables (members' individual social identities [or identity groups], current work-group composition, and change in organizational demography over an eight-year period) would influence perceptions of the diversity climate.

Individual identity-group variables. Members' individual identity-group variables such as race, gender, age, and level in the organization were believed to be strongly related to views of diversity climate. In general, white women and racioethnic men and women tend to value diversity-enlargement initiatives to a greater degree than white men (Kossek & Zonia, 1993). Although age and level were likely to be correlated, we felt it was important to include both in our model because younger and lower-level members have been found to have more favorable attitudes toward diversity activities than their senior colleagues (Kossek & Zonia, 1993). Because the current study involved a university, level was measured by whether one was tenured or not.

**Table 1. Dimensions of Diversity Climate One Would Expect to Observe
Assuming Diversity-enlargement Programs Work**

- *Members would highly value employer efforts to promote diversity.* This dimension
  is based on the premise that members would have experienced the benefits of greater
  diversity that are noted in the value-in-diversity literature. This view holds that
  diverse groups and organizations are more likely to experience increased organizational effectiveness over homogeneous organizations and groups (Cox, 1993; Cox,
  Lobel, & McLeod, 1991).

- *Members would believe senior management had a high level of commitment to
  diversity enlargement.* It is well-documented that key managers must be committed
  champions of changing the organizational efforts to promote diversity, or diversity-
  enlargement initiatives will be ephemeral at best (Morrison, 1992; Sessa, 1992).

- *Members would believe women and racioethnic minorities in their work group are
  as qualified as men and whites.* Diversity climate includes a specific component,
  which refers to the beneficiaries of change efforts who are likely to be the white
  women and the racioethnic minority men and women in one's own work unit (Kossek
  & Zonia, 1993). Perceptions toward members of these groups reflect the specific
  embodiment of the effectiveness of diversity-enlargement activities. Assuming such
  initiatives are successful, minorities and women would be less likely to be viewed as
  tokens (Kanter, 1977) in a climate highly supportive of multiculturalism than in the
  case of less favorable climates (Kossek & Zonia, 1993).

- *Members would believe the organization has done a good job of protecting the
  rights of members, such as women and minorities, and that their treatment in
  personnel decisions pertaining to advancement are fair and unbiased; and Members would believe there is equal work-group support for individuals, regardless of
  race or gender.* Diversity efforts seek to alter intergroup relations based on
  racioethnicity and gender in organizations; yet social psychological theory had shown
  that people have a predisposition to develop an in-group preference in contrast with
  other groups (Sherif, Harvey, White, Hood, & Sherif, 1961; Tajfel, 1978). Consequently, it is assumed that in organizations where diversity-enlargement activities
  have had a favorable impact on the climate, perceptions regarding the fairness of the
  distribution of rewards and resource allocation would also be favorable across racial
  and gender groups. Thus, diversity-enlargement activities would have a positive
  impact on both procedural justice (the perceived fairness of *how* decisions are made)
  and distributive justice (the fairness of the *distribution* of valued outcomes such as
  departmental resources; Shepard, Lewicki, & Minton, 1992).

- *Members would believe that their work group reflects a good mix of individuals.*
  This dimension measures the degree to which members believe their work groups'
  realities reflect the larger organization's rhetoric of diversity enlargement. Members
  would experience their own work groups as being in balance with the larger organizational system's contention that diversity-enlargement strategies are being successfully
  implemented.

- *Members would have a high level of voluntary interaction with individuals of different racioethnic backgrounds, both professionally and socially.* This dimension reflects the degree to which diversity-enlargement activities have been successful in socializing members to voluntarily seek out members whose intergroup backgrounds differ from their own. It is one thing to mandate that an organization must create diversity through hiring. However, an even more vital indication of an enhanced diversity climate is reflected in behaviors where members seek to interact socially and professionally with minority co-workers based on their own volition. We thought it was important to measure both social and professional interaction, since university departments espouse collegiality that often includes interaction in social functions held off campus. In addition, the decision to collaborate on research or teaching is often left up to individual choice.

- *Members would believe the department (work group) regularly accommodates issues related to multiculturalism and values and promotes the contributions of nontraditional individuals.* This dimension reflects the degree to which diversity-enlargement activities has resulted in the integration of group processes that accommodate multiculturalism, such as making the organization's services accessible to differentially abled customers and employees. It also includes a view that the contributions of nontraditional members are not invisible but are recognized and valued. These activities reflect that change processes related to organizational learning regarding diversity have been institutionalized (Jackson, 1992).

Two final individual-level variables pertained to relational demography. Studies indicate that employees who are different from their peers in terms of age, race, or gender are more likely to experience less favorable work attitudes and behaviors (Jackson, Brett, Sessa, Cooper, Julin, & Peyronnin, 1991; Wagner, Pfeffer, & O'Reilly, 1984). Given relational demography research's findings that individual reactions to group diversity will vary depending on whether the individual is like or unlike the remainder of the group (Tsui & O'Reilly, 1989), we also felt that the more individual members were dissimilar in race or gender from their groups the less favorable would be their perceptions of diversity climate, since they would be more likely to be viewed as tokens and experience stereotyping. The more that members are demographically distant from co-workers, the lower the degree to which they will be socially integrated into a group (see also O'Reilly, Caldwell, & Barnett, 1989), and hence the less favorable their views of diversity climate.

Work-group and organizational demography. Assuming diversity-enlargement activities are institutionalized, one might expect that perceptions of climate would be explained by group and organizational measures of structure. This supposition is based on the belief that an enhanced diversity climate would mean that organizational experiences would vary less on the basis of who one is (i.e., one's own race and gender) and more on the basis of the group and organizational context in which one worked.

The demographic composition of an employee's work group and change in the demography of his or her organization as a whole are believed to have a critical influence on diversity climate. Demography influences the potential for the amount of direct contact that is likely to occur between and within gender and racial groups. It also affects members' interpretations of the extent to which the firm is actively pursuing its espoused mission of enhancing multiculturalism (Kossek & Zonia, 1994).

Intergroup relations are embedded in organizations and are affected by the extent to which power differences between members of racial and gender groups in one's immediate work group are congruent with those reflected in the supersystem of the larger organizational context (Alderfer & Smith, 1982). When there is imbalance in intergroup power differences in one's own work group and those in the larger system, dysfunctional intergroup relations are likely to occur. Therefore, members might work in a department that has a lot of gender or racial heterogeneity that should enhance perceptions of diversity climate. Yet if their larger organizational unit is either not currently very heterogeneous or has not increased heterogeneity over time, then there is the risk that individuals may experience the diversity of their own work-group social setting as being analogous to an organizational ghetto. For example, in the private sector historically, many organizations complied with affirmative action mandates by hiring women and minorities, primarily into lower-level staff functions such as the human resources department.

In universities, white women and some minority groups such as blacks and Hispanics are underrepresented in the natural sciences and overrepresented in the social sciences (Wycliff, 1990). Thus, it was believed that the more that members were in organizational units (in this case, colleges) that had increased racial and gender heterogeneity over time and had current high levels of racial and gender heterogeneity, the more positive the climate, due to the increased opportunity for the development of favorable intergroup relations through increased exposure and social contact. Similarly, the greater the racial and gender heterogeneity of one's work group, the more favorable the diversity climate. Members would be able to have increased interaction with others who were different and consequently would develop attitudes supportive of multiculturalism.

Study Background and Method

The nineteen colleges involved in this study were part of a large public university in the Midwest. Like many U.S. employers in the early 1980s, this university embarked on an extensive diversity-enlargement strategy focused on increased recruitment and retention of women and minorities. Training to promote diversity sensitivity among administrators and faculty was also initiated, although it was implemented in a decentralized voluntary fashion so the extent of delivery varied across the organization. In addition, small cash achievement awards were available annually to recognize nominated group and college activities that increased sensitivity to promoting multiculturalism.

Despite these diversity-enlargement activities, the nature of the work conducted at the university is still primarily done in isolation. Issues of tenure and promotion are based on individual performance. Few courses are team taught, and research continues to be mainly a solo endeavor. Because acquiring support for research is considered a major criterion used in awarding tenure, the faculty are like individual entrepreneurs marketing their skills for research dollars. Applying the work of Weick (1976), universities can be seen as loosely coupled systems with individual faculty members only weakly connected to their department (vis-à-vis their teaching) and hardly connected at all to the larger organization, the college and university in which the department (the work group) is embedded. This design of jobs promotes the achievement of performance through individual rather than group activities and reduces the opportunity for members to modify attitudes through intimate experiences and interactions.

In this study, we collected data by survey and by using personnel records that spanned a period of eight years.

The Survey

After nearly a decade of implementation of diversity-enlargement activities, a random sample of all faculty members was selected and a survey was sent to them to assess diversity climate. The survey data were linked with a separate data file from the university's personnel records of the members' race and gender and eight years of change in organizational demography of members' colleges. The response rate of 775 surveys was 51% for whites and 47% for people of color. Virtually all of the respondents possessed advanced graduate degrees, most of which were Ph.D.s. Fifty-two percent were male and 48% were female; 84% of the responding sample was white, and 16% were minority-group members (8% Asian, 6% African-American, and 2% Hispanic).

After the survey was returned, an exploratory factor analysis was done to develop ten scales that could be used to assess diversity climate. For all of the scales, the lower the score, the more unfavorable the attitudes. A complete listing of the ten scales (diversity-climate measures) can be found in Appendix A, so only highlights are given here.

Attitudes toward employer efforts to promote diversity was measured using 8 items (alpha = .89). Sample items: "If organization x is to remain an excellent institution, it must recruit and retain more women faculty . . . more minority faculty . . . more disabled faculty."

Commitment of administration to diversity (alpha = .85) was measured using 5 items. A sample is: "The dean of my college is strongly committed to recruiting more minority faculty."

Fairness of organization (alpha = .69; 5 items) included the item: "It is harder for women faculty members in my department to get tenure than men."

Work-group support of multiculturalism (alpha = .81; 6 items) included the item: "Issues of diversity and pluralism are often topics of discussion in my department meetings."

The perceived *qualifications of women and minorities* scales (respective alphas .71 [2 items] and .75 [3 items]) assessed the degree to which members felt the qualifications of women and minority faculty had to be higher than those of white men.

The *equality of support for racioethnic minorities and women* scales (respective alphas .73 [3 items] and .76 [3 items]) assessed the degree to which these members had an equal chance of getting department support compared with white men.

Perceived work-group mix (alpha = .72; 5 items) included: "My department has a good mix of men and women faculty members."

Professional and social interaction with diverse members (alpha = .70; 6 items) assessed the frequency that members interacted socially and professionally with colleagues of different racioethnic backgrounds.

Personnel Records

Individuals identified their race/ethnicity, gender, age, and tenure status. A member's race and gender similarity in relation to their group was determined using Tsui and O'Reilly's (1989) measure. The higher the score, the greater the dissimilarity from the group. Using data from the personnel office, the actual representation of women and minorities from 1982 to 1990 by college, current group and organizational heterogeneity, and percent change in heterogeneity over time were assessed. Our sample had nineteen colleges with over forty thousand faculty, staff, and students, and we viewed each college as a small organizational unit. We believe this assumption is apt, given, for example, the likelihood of vast differences in racial and gender demography across colleges such as the College of Engineering compared with the College of Social Science.

Our heterogeneity measure was derived from Kossek and Zonia (1993). The higher the score, the greater the heterogeneity. Variables assessing current work-group and organization size and the change in organization size from 1982 and 1990 were also included in the model, because in smaller units, there is more opportunity for individual contact.

Analyses

Means, standard deviations for each measure, and standard correlations between them were computed. To test the hypotheses central to the study, we used two different regression strategies. Our first strategy was to use all of the independent variables to explain each of the ten measures of diversity climate. All independent variables were added at one time. Thus, the betas would represent each independent variable's unique influence on each measure of diversity climate.

Our second analytic strategy was to conduct hierarchical regression, entering blocks of individual, department, and organizational variables for each of the ten scales assessing diversity climate.

Results and Discussion

Table 2 shows means, standard deviations, and correlations for the diversity-climate measures. The sample as a whole held the most favorable views regarding the value of employer efforts to promote diversity (mean 3.73) and the least favorable views regarding the extent to which members voluntarily sought to interact with individuals of different racioethnicities (mean 2.45). The qualifications of women were viewed as being slightly higher than those of white men (mean 3.13), and the qualifications of minorities (mean 2.81) were viewed as being slightly lower than white men's. The sample was slightly favorable regarding attitudes concerning the administration's perceived commitment to diversity (3.53) and fairness of the organization (3.45). White women were viewed as having a slightly lower chance of getting equal support (1.89), and minorities were viewed as having the same chance (2.02) of getting equal support compared to white men for

Table 2. Correlation Matrix and Descriptive Statistics[1]

	Mean	SD	1	2	3	4	5	6	7	8	9	10
1. Attitudes toward Employer Efforts to Promote Diversity	3.73	.81	.89									
2. Commitment of Administration to Diversity	3.53	.80	.00	.85								
3. Perceived Qualifications of Women	3.13	.62	.23**	.18**	.71							
4. Perceived Qualifications of Racioethnic Minority Colleagues	2.81	.63	.28**	-.10	.18*	.75						
5. Fairness of Organization	3.45	.71	-.35**	.46**	-.15**	-.26**	.69					
6. Perceived Work-group Mix	3.06	.84	-.29**	.36**	-.16**	-.07	.39**	.72				
7. Equality of Support for Racioethnic Minorities	2.02	.38	.00	.33**	-.23**	-.04	.18**	.09	.73			
8. Equality of Support for Women	1.89	.38	-.02	.36**	-.07	.02	.18**	.11**	.80**	.76		
9. Social and Professional Interaction with Diverse Members	2.45	.58	-.03	.14**	.01	.08	.10	.15**	.04	.06	.70	
10. Work-group Support of Multiculturalism	2.85	.34	-.05	.49**	.01	-.06	.33**	.39**	.28**	.24**	.16**	.81

[1]alpha in diagonal
** $p < .01$

this 3-point scale. Respondents were neither favorable nor unfavorable regarding the degree to which they felt their departments had a good work-group mix, as the mean hovered near the scale's midpoint (3.06). Views were less than favorable regarding the degree to which their work group supported multiculturalism (2.85).

Table 3 summarizes the betas from the results of the regression models. Appendix B gives a text summary of the findings of our regression analyses. Due to space limitations, only highlights will be reported here. Our discussion of the findings focuses on the explanatory power of the independent variables. All of the models were significant. The models that explained the most variance (from 22% to 26%) had the dependent variables of equality of support for women, equality of support for minorities, fairness of organization, perceived work-group mix, and perceived qualifications of minorities.

Organizational-level Findings

Increasing the racial heterogeneity over time did not significantly relate to diversity climate in any of the models. We surmise that the lack of significant results related to several factors. First, although nearly all colleges have increased the numbers of minority faculty, the raw numbers of actual minority hires are still tiny. The national recruitment pool of minority Ph.D.s has not increased rapidly enough for some racioethnic groups, and the growth in openings in the 1980s was not enough to allow the institution we studied to hire large numbers of minorities (DePalma, 1988). Furthermore, the presence of various racioethnic minorities across the university is likely to be uneven. For example, individuals of Asian ethnicity are better represented than blacks or Hispanics in the natural sciences (Wycliff, 1990). In addition, there is likely to be ambiguity in the minds of the faculty over what constitutes a minority. Hiring a Ph.D. from India or Asia or one of Indian or Asian-American descent is not likely to be psychologically experienced in the same way by many faculty as hiring an African-American Ph.D., given the history of extreme prejudice toward blacks in the United States.

Increasing the gender heterogeneity over time was only significantly related to diversity climate in one model. It had a negative relationship to perceptions of minority qualifications, suggesting increasing negative inter-group competitive dynamics (see Blalock, 1967) as the female group increased in a college. Perhaps increasing the representation of women in organizations without concomitant increases in racial heterogeneity over time (since colleges have generally hired greater numbers of women [often white] than minorities) may marginalize minority members by fostering stereotyping

Table 3. Summary of Regression Models[4]

VARIABLES	Attitudes toward Employer Efforts to Promote Diversity	Commitment of Administration to Diversity	Perceived Qualifications of Women	Perceived Qualifications of Racioethnic Minorities	Fairness of Organization	Perceived Work-group Mix	Equality of Support for Racioethnic Minorities	Equality of Support for Women	Social and Professional Interaction with Diverse Members	Work-group Support of Multiculturalism
INDIVIDUAL LEVEL										
Racioethnicity[1]	-.16	.15	-.12	-1.07***	.31***	-.76***	.30*	-.13	-.50***	-.17
Gender[2]	-.20**	.09	-.25***	-.06	.29***	.15*	.12*	.49***	.09	.08
Job Security[3]	.03	.03	.00	-.08	.09*	-.10*	.06	.03	-.01	-.10*
Age	.02	.07	.00	.00	.12***	.04	.02	.01	.01	.06
Race Dissimilarity	.06	.06	-.23	-.94***	.16	-1.03***	-.02	-.31*	-.41*	-.24
Gender Dissimilarity	.18**	-.21**	-.03	.05	-.11	-.20**	-.18*	.02	-.06	-.17*
GROUP LEVEL (Department)										
Gender Heterogeneity	.03	.22***	-.04	-.16**	.08	.16**	.12	-.04	.22***	.21**
Race Heterogeneity	-.05	-.04	.16*	.36***	.02	.61***	-.02	-.23**	.06	.18*
Group Size	.00	-.03	-.09	.01	-.04	-.03	-.03	.11*	.02	.07
ORGANIZATION LEVEL (College)										
1. Change in Size 1982-90	.02	.16*	.10	-.03	.14*	.07	.04	.10	.12*	.08
2. Organization Size	-.02	-.14**	.06	.03	-.06	-.07	-.13*	-.15**	-.09	-.15**
3. Change in Race Heterogeneity 1982-90	.00	-.08	.02	.00	.07	-.01	-.04	.03	-.07	-.01
4. Race Heterogeneity	.03	-.15*	-.17*	-.06	-.19**	-.26***	-.09	-.30***	.08	-.29***
5. Change in Gender Heterogeneity 1982-90	.18	-.15	.14	-.33***	.00	-.10	.04	-.12	.04	-.13
6. Gender Heterogeneity	.19*	-.11	.15	.02	-.09	.11	-.14	-.12	-.09	-.09
TOTAL R^2	.19	.11	.12	.23	.22	.23	.22	.26	.10	.10
TOTAL MODEL F	8.13***	4.16***	4.40***	9.37***	9.73***	10.20***	8.95***	11.86***	3.79***	3.64***

[1]1=white, 0=minority; [2]1=male, 0=female; [3]1=secure, 0=non-secure; [4]Betas shown for each model

and tokenism, which lower perceptions of their qualifications. In sum, measures to implement diversity-enlargement strategies over time were not positively linked to climate.

Although changing racial and gender heterogeneity did not have a positive impact on climate, refuting our *Hypothesis 1,* surprisingly *increasing the college size* did in three models. The greater the college growth, the more positive the attitudes regarding the administration's commitment to diversity, the fairness of the organization, and the extent of reported social and professional interaction among individuals of different ethnicities. Increasing size allows a college to hire new faculty and change its racioethnic and gender composition through growth, not downsizing. Perhaps units that were allowed to grow were able to staff new positions with minorities and females, thereby allowing them to meet university mandates favoring increasing diversity. Although growth in size was positively linked to climate, *size in and of itself* had a negative impact on climate in four models. Individuals in large units were less likely to believe the administration was committed to diversity, that women and minorities got equal support, or that their work group supported multiculturalism. Perhaps if one works in a college that is too large, efforts to enhance diversity may be diluted in impact. Large colleges may have to spread resources and initiatives across larger numbers of faculty compared to smaller departments.

An unfavorable relationship to climate was found for the *current racial heterogeneity at the college level.* The higher the current college racial heterogeneity, the more negative the attitudes regarding the administration's commitment to diversity, the perceived qualifications of women, the fairness of the organization, the perceived work-group mix, the equality of support for women, and the degree to which one's work group supported multiculturalism. These findings also support competition theories of social dynamics pertaining to the notion that given a fixed amount of resources, increasing a minority group's size heightens negative competitive dynamics with other organizational groups (Blalock, 1967).

Increasing *gender heterogeneity at the college level* had little impact on the diversity climate variables, although it was positively related to perceptions supporting employer efforts to promote diversity. One explanation for these results is that the negative dynamics described by intergroup theories of competition may be more likely to surface in regard to racial heterogeneity as opposed to gender heterogeneity. Perhaps white men are less threatened by increasing the representation of women (typically white) than by increasing the representation of minority men and women. Or perhaps it is due to the fact that colleges have had longer experience with and been able to hire larger numbers of women than minorities. Currently, white women are substantially better represented at the Ph.D. level than racioethnic minorities (DePalma, 1988). In contrast, the increase in minority faculty representation has not kept up with the increase in minority student enrollment (Porras, 1991).

Work Group- (Department-) level Findings

Turning to the work-group or department level, *current work-group gender heterogeneity* was significant in five models, while *group racial heterogeneity* was significant in four models. The greater the current gender and racial heterogeneity of the work group, the more respondents felt they had a good mix and that their work group supported multiculturalism. Gender heterogeneity was also positively linked to favorable attitudes regarding the extent of research and teaching interaction with individuals of different racioethnicities and the perceived commitment of the administration to diversity. However, gender heterogeneity was negatively related to perceptions of minority qualifications, which suggests that a significant amount of gender diversity may lower the perceived degree of racial diversity perhaps resulting in the existing minority colleagues being viewed as tokens. Or perhaps the greater the gender heterogeneity, the more the heightening of competitive win-lose intergroup dynamics between gender and racial groups.

Department race heterogeneity was also significantly related to positive views toward the qualifications of minorities, but negatively related to a belief that women got equal support as men. *Group size* was generally not significantly related to climate. Although the results are slightly mixed in that some competitive dynamics between white women and minorities emerge with increasing department heterogeneity, unlike the college-level findings which were virtually consistently negative, it appears that there is a positive relationship between some indicators of diversity climate and the greater the heterogeneity at the work-group (department) level.

Individual-level Findings

Of the individual-level variables, *gender* and *gender dissimilarity* were significantly related to diversity climate in five of the ten models. Men were less likely to believe that women were qualified and more likely to believe that resource support to women and minorities was equal, that their work group had a good mix, and that the organization was fair. The more that one was dissimilar in gender to work-group members, the more an individual valued diversity, but the less likely he or she viewed the administration as being committed to diversity, believed the work group had a good mix, provided equal support for minorities, or supported multiculturalism.

Race was significant in four models. Whites were less likely to view minorities as qualified, less likely to think their department had a good demographic mix, and less likely to seek out interactions with minorities, but felt the organization was fair. *Race dissimilarity* was a significant predictor of diversity climate for four models. The less similar the individual was in race to the group, the lower the perceptions of minorities' qualifications and the favorableness of the work-group mix, the equality of support for women, and the level of voluntary interaction with minorities. It appears that the more one is in a token status for race, the less favorable the relationship to climate.

Finally, *age* and *tenure* did not explain much variance in the models, other than being significantly positively related to perceiving the organization as fair.

Summary of Hierarchical Regression Analysis
Separate hierarchical regressions entering blocks of individual, department, and organizational variables were conducted for the ten scales assessing diversity climate. (Here we briefly summarize the results of these analyses; details are available from the first author.) Our use of blocks reflected our belief that groups of variables could be entered in the order of their likelihood to have the greatest influence on one's experiences and attitudes pertaining to diversity issues. Specifically, respondent's personal demographics were believed to have a greater immediate impact on attitudes regarding diversity climate than environmental variables. Thus, individual variables were entered first, since it has been found that individual social identities have the greatest influence on diversity climate (Kossek & Zonia, 1993). The next variables entered were those relating to the demography of one's own department, since one's work group is likely to have a greater impact on day-to-day social interactions than the demography of one's college, which was entered last.

The hierarchical regression analysis showed that individual-level variables explained significantly more of the variance in nine out of ten regressions than group and organizational contextual variables. Despite the fact that the first block entered nearly always has a greater potential to explain more of the variance, organizational-level variables (entered as the third block) significantly added to the variance explained in nine of the ten models, while the block of work-group variables was significant in five models. Work-group variables explained the most variance for the perceived work-group mix model, which was the only model where a demographic block of variables related to structure explained more variance than an individual-level block. Thus, our results showed that while individual variables are the best predictors of diversity climate, organizational demography at both the group and organizational level significantly adds to the variance explained.

General Discussion and Conclusions

Our study shows that simply increasing racial and gender diversity in organizations and work groups is not sufficient to promote a favorable diversity climate. These results are in line with research by Alderfer and Smith (1982) concerning the embeddedness of intergroup relations in organizational contexts and the importance of balance in power dynamics at both the group level and within the larger organizational system. If the heterogeneity of one's work group is perceived as being out of balance in relation to the diversity reflected in the larger organizational context, negative social dynamics may occur. Our findings are also consistent with a study by Ely (1994), where it was found that organizations need gender representation at the top of the organization in order to reap the benefits of added gender diversity at lower levels. The administration (deans and department chairs) of the nineteen colleges studied were predominantly white and male.

Given the changing demographics of the U.S. labor force, few organizations today will have great difficulty in hiring a diverse group of employees, particularly for lower-level positions. What organizations will have difficulty with is managing diversity to effectively capitalize on it for the benefit of the organization (Thomas, 1990). It is one thing to hire people who differ in background from the current employee mix; it is quite another to create a work environment where members value and respect the views of those who are different, seek out and enjoy interacting with a wide variety of individuals, and work productively in those relationships (Kossek & Zonia, 1993). And ironically, for years organizations have designed their systems to promote uniformity of behavior from employees.

Like the organization in this study, most diversity-enlargement strategies are implemented in concert with a color-blind approach that ignores cultural differences and expects diverse newcomers to conform to a homogeneous culture (Ferdman, 1989). However, many employees today are unwilling to suppress their cultural and ethnic differences and those who do risk incurring the potential costs of added stress and lower performance (Cox,

1993). In addition, forcing assimilation may also result in organizations losing some of the benefits they hope to reap from diversity, as minority members may mask their uniqueness by changing their behavior to fit with the dominant culture.

Diversity for What Purpose?

We have shown that simply increasing organizational diversity is not sufficient to make the organizational-climate changes we believe organizations are interested in making in order to reap some of the benefits of diversity, such as increased creativity, breadth, and increased adaptability to diverse markets, among others (for a discussion of the value of diversity, see Cox & Blake, 1991). In the diversity literature on organizational efforts to enhance diversity, a problem we have observed is that organizations have not been really clear about the specific benefits they seek to gain from increasing diversity. For some firms, is increasing diversity an end in itself? If it is, the question is, How do organizations increase diversity without losing other benefits of a homogeneous employee population such as consistency in organizational values, current productivity, and quality levels? This is the perspective Thomas (1990) seems to offer in some of his work concerning the need to manage diversity to organizational advantage.

Other organizations seem to want to increase productivity and quality through diversity, such as the case at Corning cited in Morrison, Ruderman, and Hughes-James (1993). Still others, and perhaps most organizations, really aren't completely sure of the organizational objectives they hope to achieve by enhancing diversity; they just know that they should, or by virtue of what is available in the labor market, have to have a more diverse workforce.

Yet most of the jobs available to this increasingly diverse workforce are predominantly at the lower level. In the current study, we examined the attitudes of a faculty, where most candidates considered to be qualified are white (particularly tenured faculty) and predominantly male. Related to this dilemma is the question of whether our climate measure of enhancing intergroup social interaction should be a professional goal if different racial groups rarely mix outside of the workplace, unless they are from similar socioeconomic classes. Is the workplace a microcosm of the external society or the reverse? Should the workplace be used as a lever to improve social interaction across social-identity groups? Organizations have failed to clearly identify the links between human resource strategies to increase diversity, diversity climate, and organizational outcomes.

Coupling Diversity Initiatives with Teamwork

Our study has shown that organizational demographic approaches focused on diversity enlargement are necessary but insufficient strategies for fostering employee attitudes highly supportive of workplace diversity. We believe that diversity-enlargement strategies are most likely to succeed if they also include group-based change approaches that are devised to alter the design of jobs, the structure of the workplace, and the supporting reward systems in a manner that fosters collaboration, mentoring, voluntary role modeling, and other forms of intergroup teamwork. Intergroup-based interventions are important because member attitudes don't change in a vacuum. Social contact is insufficient for enhancing diversity climate; the contact must be structured toward the collaborative achievement of work-related tasks.

Individual attitudes are embedded in terms of what members see and experience through interaction with colleagues of different backgrounds. Because each person is viewed as a group representative, every individual's group memberships can influence interactions with other groups (Alderfer, 1977). The organization must offer and reward participation in activities focused on work-related tasks that are designed to increase intimacy, reduce cultural distance, and heighten perceived similarity and attraction among intergroup members (see also Triandis et al., 1994). In this way, the interventions go much further than diversity-enlargement approaches. If an organization is going to create a vital multicultural environment, then the work cannot be done in isolation, or even in homogeneous groups, and the organizational system must reinforce multicultural group efforts focused on the achievement of primary organizational objectives. Examples of such activities in educational institutions might be organizational support of team-teaching, team and dyadic research projects on topics where diversity is important for increased understanding, internal task forces on internal organizational problems, teams focused on student recruitment and alumni relations, and service-outreach oriented consulting projects geared to improving the knowledge base of important external constituents. Yet like many employers, the organization in the current study initiated diversity-enlargement activities that overlooked the potential of team-based interventions for improving diversity climate and overrelied on the strategy of altering organizational demography as a vehicle for organizational change. This latter strategy creates diversity without necessarily providing opportunities for positive interaction among intergroup members. We hope that future research will investigate the following relationship:

Human Resource Strategies (diversity enlargement + intergroup teamwork)	$\longrightarrow$	Enhanced Diversity Climate	$\longrightarrow$	Positive Organizational Outcomes (e.g., enhanced profitability, quality)

Although not specifically examined in this study, we would like to note that another commonly employed human resource strategy, *diversity sensitivity*, acknowledges the existence of cultural distance and attempts to teach individual members about cultural differences through training (Ferdman, 1989). Yet accentuating dissimilarity will not necessarily increase positive intergroup attitudes. It may, in fact, even inhibit them when conducted as isolated events that promote stereotyping and labeling. Rather, interventions that result in the heightening of perceptions of similarity and mutual attraction (Triandis et al., 1994) such as intergroup teamwork must also occur.

Limitations of this Study

As with any study there are limitations, which we hope will be improved upon in future research. We believe our measures of racial dissimilarity (the degree to which one is different from group members) and racial heterogeneity (the degree to which a group is ethnically diverse) need to be improved upon by developing measures that do not operationalize race as a dichotomous variable (e.g., white/people of color). It is possible that our results for the racial heterogeneity variables and the racial dissimilarity variables would be different if we had computed race in a way that allows for the examination of differences within the minority group, such as that advocated by Tsui, Eagan, and O'Reilly (1992). Their approach enables the computation of relational measures in a manner that allows for the proportional consideration of racial differences, which we hope to further explore with our data.

The racioethnic composition of the sample respondents who were people of color, while reflective of the racial demography of most academic institutions of higher education, is another influence on our results. Half of our minority sample were Asian or Pacific Islander, and the attitudes of members of these groups may be more similar to whites than those of African-Americans and Hispanics (Kossek & Zonia, 1994). There is also no way to assess what portion of our sample is foreign born, and the attitude of individuals who grew up outside of America is likely to systematically differ from those who grew up in the U.S.

The distribution of differences may have affected our results, also. Specifically, our conclusions about gender are based on results from a sample that was very evenly split (48% female and 52% male), and there was a good deal of variance across colleges. In contrast, our sample was predominantly white (84%), which limited the variance of our racial dissimilarity and heterogeneity measures. Consequently, our results for gender heterogeneity may do a better job of measuring diversity climate effects than our racial measures, even though the proportion of these measures are reflective of most faculties in the U.S., where most candidates considered qualified are mainly white and often male.

Although there are situations in our sample where women could be similar in gender to their group, there were probably no cases when minorities were similar to other members of their work group. This limited variance is one of the problems researchers face when studying racial dynamics in many professional and managerial organizations. We also believe we need to do more research that focuses on the interactions between race, gender, and level, since some of the effects such as negative reactions for being a token representative of a group have been found to exist for white men, but not as much for other members (see Tsui, Eagan, & O'Reilly, 1992). We need to further explore the differences between minority women and white women on measures regarding race, since research has shown that white women tend to be more similar to white men than to minority women on issues of racial prejudice (Van Steenberg, 1983).

Another shortcoming relates to the fact our attitudinal data is cross-sectional from one survey administration and ideally it would be beneficial to measure diversity climate with longitudinal data. We are unable to decipher the causality between individual and organizational phenomena; we simply know whether a relationship exists, but cannot necessarily say that the change in demography changed attitudes. Longitudinal data would also help us to explore whether over time there is a decrease in variance explained from individual-based demographics on diversity climate. One would expect that if a climate is truly changed, there would be more agreement on the existing diversity climate between similar work group and organizational members regardless of their own personal background.

Lastly, our belief that diversity-enlargement initiatives must be coupled with interventions aimed toward fostering teamwork are merely speculative. Although we know that increasing numbers as an isolated strategy is insufficient by itself, we don't know whether teamwork among diverse members will actually enhance climate, since no teamwork initiatives were implemented in the organization we studied. Further research is needed to identify conditions where collaboration may be necessary to establish a positive diversity climate. For example, what is the impact of diversity enlargement on teamwork in organizations where the work is essentially done alone? Could there be a positive diversity climate in such situations?

Conclusion

Despite the fact that many academicians have been outspoken supporters of the growing need of employers to better manage diversity and promote multicultural environments, universities could be viewed as lagging behind business organizations in redesigning the organization to support diversity. We believe that a critical human-resource strategy that has been lacking is the redesign of systems to support intergroup teamwork geared toward enhancing group and organizational performance. Over the long run, we theorize that such an approach is likely to be more effective than diversity-enlargement efforts in fostering positive interactions with diverse members. As this study shows, simply increasing organizational diversity is not sufficient to enhance the climate for diversity.

References

Alderfer, C. P. (1977). Group and intergroup relations. In J. R. Hackman & J. L. Suttle (Eds.), *Improving life at work: Behavioral sciences approaches to organizational change.* Santa Monica, CA: Goodyear.

Alderfer, C. P., & Smith, K. K. (1982). Studying embedded intergroup relations in organizations. *Administrative Science Quarterly, 27,* 35-65.

Allport, G. (1954). *The nature of prejudice.* Reading, MA: Addison-Wesley.

Blalock, H. M. (1967). *Toward a theory of minority group relations.* New York: Wiley.

Cox, T. (1993). *Cultural diversity in organizations: Theory, research, and practice.* San Francisco: Berrett-Koehler.

Cox, T., & Blake, S. (1991). Managing cultural diversity: Implications for organizational competitiveness. *The Executive, 5*(3), 34-47.

Cox, T., Lobel, S., & McLeod, P. (1991). Effects of ethnic group cultural difference on cooperative versus competitive behavior on a group task. *Academy of Management Journal, 34,* 827-847.

DePalma, A. (1988). *Digest of education statistics.* U.S. Department of Education: National Center for Education Statistics, Washington, DC.

Ely, R. (1994). The effects of organizational demographics and social identity on relationships among professional women. *Administrative Science Quarterly, 39,* 203-238.

Ferdman, B. (1989). Affirmative action and the challenge of the color-blind perspective. In F. A. Blanchard & F. Crosby (Eds.), *Affirmative action in perspective* (pp. 169-176). New York: Springer-Verlag.

Fernandez, J. P. (1991). *Managing a diverse workforce: Regaining the competitive edge.* Lexington, MA: D.C. Heath.

Jackson, S. E. (1992). Stepping into the future: Guidelines for action. In S. E. Jackson (Ed.), *Diversity in the workplace: Human resources initiatives* (pp. 319-339). New York: Guilford Press.

Jackson, S. E., Brett, J. F., Sessa, V. I., Cooper, D. M., Julin, J. A., & Peyronnin, K. (1991). Some differences make a difference: Individual dissimilarity and group heterogeneity as correlates of recruitment, promotions and turnover. *Journal of Applied Psychology, 75*(5), 675-689.

Kanter, R. M. (1977). Some effects of proportion on group life: Skewed sex ratios and responses to token women. *American Journal of Sociology, 5,* 965-990.

Kossek, E. E., & Zonia, S. C. (1993). Assessing diversity climate: A field study of reactions to employer efforts to promote diversity. *Journal of Organizational Behavior, 14,* 61-81.

Kossek, E. E., & Zonia, S. C. (1994). The effects of race and ethnicity on perceptions of human resource policies and climate regarding diversity. *Journal of Business and Technical Communication, 8,* 319-334.

Morrison, A. M. (1992). *The new leaders: Guidelines on leadership diversity in America.* San Francisco: Jossey-Bass.

Morrison, A. M., Ruderman, M. N., & Hughes-James, M. (1993). *Making diversity happen: Controversies and solutions.* Greensboro, NC: Center for Creative Leadership.

O'Reilly, C. A., Caldwell, D., & Barnett, W. P. (1989). Work group demography, social integration and turnover. *Administrative Science Quarterly, 34,* 21-37.

Porras, J. (1991, August). *Racism in a research university: Some observations and comments.* Paper presented at the Task Force on the Status of Minorities: Racism in International Settings. Annual meeting of the National Academy of Management, Miami, Florida.

Schneider, B., & Reichers, A. E. (1983). On the etiology of climates. *Personnel Psychology, 36,* 19-39.

Sessa, V. (1992). Managing diversity at Xerox Corporation: Balanced workforce goals and caucus groups. In S. E. Jackson (Ed.), *Diversity in the workplace: Human resources initiatives* (pp. 37-64). New York: Guilford Press.

Shepard, B. H., Lewicki, R. J., & Minton, J. W. (1992). *Organizational justice: The search for fairness in the workplace.* New York: Lexington.

Sherif, M., Harvey, O. J., White, B. J., Hood, W. R., & Sherif, C. W. (1961). *Intergroup conflict and cooperation: The robber's cave experiment.* Norman, OK: University of Oklahoma Press.

Tajfel, H. (1978). *Differentiation between social groups: Studies in the social psychology of intergroup relations.* New York: Academic Press.

Thomas, R. (1990, March-April). From affirmative action to affirming diversity. *Harvard Business Review,* pp. 107-117.

Triandis, H. C., Kurowski, L. K., & Gelfand, M. J. (1994). Workplace diversity. In H. M. Triandis, M. Dunnette, and L. Hough (Eds.), *Handbook of industrial and organizational psychology* (Vol. 4, 2nd ed., pp. 769-827). Palo Alto, CA: Consulting Psychologists Press.

Tsui, A., Eagan, T., & O'Reilly, C. (1992). Being different: Relational demography and organizational attachment. *Administrative Science Quarterly, 37,* 549-579.

Tsui, A., & O'Reilly, C. (1989). Beyond simple demographic effects: The importance of relational demography in superior-subordinate relationships. *Academy of Management Journal, 32,* 402-423.

Van Steenberg, V. (1983). Within white group differences in race relations at CTCGS. Yale School of Organization and Management Working Paper, cited in Alderfer, C. P. (1986), An intergroup perspective on group dynamics. In J. W. Lorsch (Ed.), *Handbook of organizational behavior* (pp. 190-222). Englewood Cliffs, NJ: Prentice Hall.

Wagner, W., Pfeffer, J., & O'Reilly, C. (1984). Organizational demography and turnover in top management groups. *Administrative Science Quarterly, 29,* 24-82.

Weick, K. (1976, March). Educational organizations as loosely-coupled systems. *Administrative Science Quarterly, 21,* 1-19.

Wycliff, D. (1990, June 8). Blacks advance slow in science careers. *The New York Times,* A1.

Appendix A
Scales Constructed for Study

ATTITUDES TOWARD EMPLOYER EFFORTS
TO PROMOTE DIVERSITY

(5-point scale: 5=strongly agree, 4=agree, 3=neither agree or disagree, 2=disagree, 1=strongly disagree)

If organization x is to remain an excellent institution it must recruit and retain more minority faculty.

If organization x is to remain an excellent institution it must recruit and retain more women faculty.

If organization x is to remain an excellent institution it must recruit and retain more handicapper faculty.

Increasing gender diversity among the faculty is important in promoting greater understanding and cooperation between men and women.

Increasing minority representation among the faculty is an important way to achieve multi-racial understanding and cooperation.

The organization should continue to work toward ensuring that academic programs are fully accessible to handicappers.

Recognition of differences in sexual orientation should be included in all organizational documents concerning diversity on campus.

Greater understanding and cooperation of individuals with different sexual orientations is fostered by the presence of gay and lesbian scholars and students in the university community.

ATTITUDES TOWARD MINORITY QUALIFICATIONS

(5-point scale: 5=much higher, 4=slightly higher, 3=about the same, 2=slightly lower, 1=much lower)

The scholarly qualifications of minority faculty compared to nonminority faculty in my school/department are _____.

The research productivity of minority faculty compared to nonminority faculty in my school/department is _____.

ATTITUDES TOWARD FEMALE QUALIFICATIONS

(5-point scale: 5=much higher, 4=slightly higher, 3=about the same, 2=slightly lower, 1=much lower)

Research productivity of women faculty compared to men faculty in my school/
department is ____.

The scholarly qualifications of women faculty as compared to men faculty in my
school/department are ____.

EQUALITY OF DEPARTMENT SUPPORT OF MINORITIES

(3-point scale: 3=better chance, 2=same chance, 1=less chance)

Compared to nonminority faculty, minority faculty have ____ of having graduate
students to assist them.

Compared to nonminority faculty, minority faculty have ____ of getting a release
from teaching.

Compared to nonminority faculty, minority faculty have ____ of receiving salary
increases above the average merit rate.

EQUALITY OF DEPARTMENT SUPPORT OF WOMEN

(3-point scale: 3=better chance, 2=same chance, 1=less chance)

Compared to faculty men, faculty women have ____ of having graduate students
to assist them.

Compared to faculty men, faculty women have ____ of getting a release from
teaching.

Compared to faculty men, faculty women have ____ of receiving salary increases
above the average merit rate.

SOCIAL/PROFESSIONAL INTERACTION WITH
DIVERSE INDIVIDUALS

(4-point scale: 4=very often, 3=often, 2=seldom, 1=never or almost never)

How often do you interact socially with colleagues?
How often do social interactions include colleagues with racial/ethnic backgrounds different from your own?
How often do you collaborate on research with colleagues?
How often does this collaboration include colleagues with racial/ethnic backgrounds different from your own?
How often do you collaborate on teaching courses with colleagues?
How often does teaching collaboration include colleagues with racial/ethnic backgrounds different from your own?

COMMITMENT OF ADMINISTRATION TO DIVERSITY

(5-point scale: 5=strongly agree, 4=agree, 3=neither agree or disagree, 2=disagree, 1=strongly disagree)

The Dean of my college is strongly committed to recruiting more minority faculty.
The Chair of my unit is strongly committed to recruiting more minority faculty.
The Dean of my college is strongly committed to increasing the gender diversity of the faculty.
The Chair of my unit is strongly committed to increasing the gender diversity of the faculty.
The Chair of my department appreciates time I spend fostering multicultural understanding and cooperation.

FAIRNESS OF ORGANIZATION

(5-point scale: 5=strongly agree, 4=agree, 3=neither agree or disagree, 2=disagree, 1=strongly disagree)

It is harder for women faculty members in my department to get tenure than men.

It is harder for minority faculty in my department to get tenure than nonminority faculty.

The university-level administration has established as a high priority promotion of multi-racial understanding and cooperation.

The university has done a good job of making the campus accessible to handicappers.

The university has done a good job of protecting the rights of gay and lesbian students and faculty.

PERCEIVED WORK-GROUP MIX

(5-point scale: 5=strongly agree, 4=agree, 3=neither agree or disagree, 2=disagree, 1=strongly disagree)

Minority graduate students are well represented in my department.

My department has a good mix of men and women faculty members.

Women graduate students are well represented in my department.

Minority faculty members are well represented in my department.

My department offers students faculty role models of the same gender and race.

WORK GROUP SUPPORT OF MULTICULTURALISM

(5-point scale: 5=strongly agree, 4=agree, 3=neither agree or disagree, 2=disagree, 1=strongly disagree)

Issues of diversity and pluralism are topics of discussion in my department meetings.

My department chair has assisted me in securing resources necessary for handicapper students that I have had in my courses.

My department has made accommodations for handicapper faculty.

My department has a mentoring program for minority and/or women faculty.

The curriculum in my department highlights the contributions made to the field by minority faculty.

The curriculum in my department highlights the contributions made to the field by handicapper faculty.

The curriculum in my department highlights the contributions made to the field by women faculty.

Appendix B
Text Summary of Key Findings from Regressions of Individual, Group, and Organizational Demographic Predictors of Diversity Climate Measures

INDIVIDUAL-LEVEL FINDINGS

1. *Whites* are less likely to view racioethnic minority colleagues as qualified, more likely to view the organization as fair and believe that minorities get at least the same level of department support as whites, less likely to think their work group has a good mix, and less likely to interact professionally or socially with people who differ in background.

2. *Men* are less likely to value organizational efforts to enhance diversity, less likely to view female colleagues as qualified, more likely to believe women and racioethnic minorities receive at least the same level of support as men and whites, more likely to perceive the organization as being fair, and more likely to think their work group has a good mix.

3. *Tenured* or job secure faculty and professional staff are more likely to view the organization as fair, but less likely to think their department has a good mix, or supports multiculturalism.

4. *The less similar one is to other department members on race*, the less likely the individual perceives minorities to have ͇qual qualifications to whites, the less likely one believes one's work group has a good mix, the less likely one thinks women get at least the same level of support as men, and the less likely one interacts socially or professionally with people who differ in background.

5. *The less similar one is to other department members on gender*, the more positive one's attitudes toward employer efforts to promote diversity, but the less one believes the administration is committed to diversity, the less one believes their work group has a good mix or supports multiculturalism, and that minorities get at least the same level of support as whites.

GROUP-LEVEL (DEPARTMENT) FINDINGS

6. *The greater the gender heterogeneity of the department*, the more likely one believes the administration is committed to diversity, the more likely one believes their department has a good mix and supports multiculturalism, the more likely one interacts socially and professionally with people who differ

in background, and the less likely one believes minority colleagues have the same qualifications as whites.

7. *The greater the racial heterogeneity of the department*, the more likely one believes minorities and women are qualified, that their work group has a good mix and supports multiculturalism, and that women get at least the same level of support as men.

8. *The larger an employee's department,* the more likely one believes women get equal levels of support as their male colleagues.

ORGANIZATIONAL-LEVEL (COLLEGE) FINDINGS

9. *The greater the increase in college size over time,* the greater the perceived commitment of the administration to diversity, the more that the organization is viewed as fair, and the greater the professional and social interaction with people who differ in background.

10. *The larger an employee's college,* the less likely one believes the administration is committed to diversity, that women and minorities get at least the same level of support as men and whites, or that their work group supports multiculturalism.

11. *Increasing a college's racial heterogeneity over time* had no significant effects on diversity climate.

12. *Increasing a college's gender heterogeneity over time* was negatively related to holding positive attitudes toward the qualifications of racioethnic minorities.

13. *The greater a college's racial heterogeneity*, the lower the perceived commitment of the administration to diversity, the lower the perceived fairness of the organization, the lower the attitudes toward women's qualifications, the less likely one believed their work group had a good mix or supported multiculturalism, and the less likely one believed women got at least the same level of support as men.

14. *The greater a college's gender heterogeneity,* the more favorable the attitudes toward employer efforts to enhance diversity.

THE DYNAMICS OF
GROUP PROCESS

THE VICIOUS AND VIRTUOUS FACETS OF WORKFORCE DIVERSITY

Sumita Raghuram
Management Systems Department
Graduate School of Business Administration
Fordham University

Raghu Garud
Stern School of Business
New York University

Abstract

Diversity, a key reality of our everyday work lives, can provoke two different outcomes. The virtuous outcome is when diversity enhances a group's ability to be cohesive and productive. The vicious outcome is when diversity detracts from a group's ability to create something that is greater than the sum of its parts. This paper adopts a process perspective to explore how these two outcomes arise. First, it explores conditions under which workforce diversity enhances group cohesion and productivity. Next, it examines mechanisms that drive a group's evolution over time and suggests how group interactions can initiate vicious and virtuous cycles. Implications for theory and practice are discussed.

✳ ✳ ✳

Diversity has the potential of bringing out the best and the worst in people. Some people value and cultivate diversity; others detest and discourage it. Organizations find themselves caught in the middle trying to balance the benefits of increased productivity and new ideas on the one hand and the costs of conflict and dissatisfaction on the other. As a result, two questions gain importance: Which facets of diversity lead to group cohesion and productivity? and, What are the dynamics that unfold from diversity?

We thank Arun Kumaraswamy and Sanjay Jain for their comments on an earlier version of this paper.

The basic thesis of this paper is that group cohesion and productivity are affected by diversity in two interrelated work arenas—the *technical arena,* comprised of task-related skills and knowledge; and the *institutional arena,* comprised of work-related values. We propose that diversity of skills in the technical arena can lead to positive outcomes and diversity of values in the institutional arena can lead to negative outcomes. The interaction of these two dimensions can result in a group becoming either cohesive and productive or fractious and unproductive. We label the dynamics that lead to these outcomes as being *virtuous* and *vicious* cycles, respectively.

The paper is organized as follows. Beginning with a brief review of the literature on diversity, we suggest that groups are more likely to be cohesive and productive if they have diverse skills in the technical arena and similar values in the institutional arena. We then adopt a process perspective to explore the mechanisms that increase or decrease diversity in these two arenas. Identification of these mechanisms provides a way to appreciate how vicious cycles are created and how process interventions can shape a group's evolution toward a virtuous cycle. In conclusion, we consider the implications of our process model for theory, research, and practice.

Literature on Workforce Diversity

Researchers have looked at diversity from several disciplinary perspectives. Those who have studied it in the marketplace have explored how product variety can enhance consumer welfare (e.g., Friedman & Friedman, 1980). Others, who have studied cultural diversity, have explored the effect of dissimilar values, norms, and beliefs on group cohesion and conflict (e.g., Brislin, 1981; Triandis, 1984). At a more microlevel of analysis, researchers have examined how diversity leads to different perceptions about group phenomena resulting in the formation of in-groups and out-groups (e.g., Ferdman, 1992; Kanter, 1977a, 1977b).

Common to these different perspectives is an appreciation that diversity can have both positive and negative outcomes. On the positive side, for instance, heterogeneous teams have been found to bring multiple perspectives to tasks, and as a result, outperform homogeneous teams in generating ideas (Filley, House, & Kerr, 1976; Hoffman, 1979; McGrath, 1984). Similarly, diversity of functional backgrounds of top-management teams has been associated with organizational innovation (Bantel & Jackson, 1989; Finkelstein & Hambrick, 1990).

On the negative side, researchers have found that diversity generates higher turnover rates because it inhibits the development of strong affective ties among group members (Jackson, Brett, Sessa, Cooper, Julin, & Peyronnin, 1991; O'Reilly, Caldwell, & Barnett, 1989; Wagner, Pffefer, & O'Reilly, 1984). Stereotyping is another deleterious consequence of diversity (Jackson, Stone, & Alvarez, 1993; Kanter, 1977a, 1977b). Jackson et al. (1993) suggest that diversity makes social identities more salient, thereby triggering stereotyping as personal identities become submerged.

In addition to examining the outcomes of diversity, researchers have explored its antecedents. These include changes in: (1) the global competitive environment, (2) the workplace, and (3) society (e.g., Johnston & Packer, 1987). For instance, globalization, a characteristic of about seventy percent of all U.S. firms, requires sensitivity to different cultural patterns and value systems. In the workplace, workforce composition has changed over time and now includes a greater proportion of older workers, white women, people of color, and immigrants. Changing societal values on diversity also create challenges for organizations as they attempt to meet diverse employee requirements, provide a prejudice-free workplace, and deal with issues such as sexual harassment.

Jackson, May, and Whitney (1995) propose a framework that links antecedents with consequences of diversity. They suggest that elements of diversity affect *mediating states*, such as cognition, affect, status, and power, leading to certain short- and long-term behaviors. Short-term behaviors include communication, social influence, and management of human resources. These behaviors, in turn, affect long-term behaviors, such as task performance and interpersonal relationships.

In contemporary environments characterized by rapid change and complexity, distinctions between antecedents, consequences, and mediating states begin to blur. In such environments, diversity (or the lack of it) grows exponentially to result in further diversity or similarity. In the process, group interactions lead to a set of dynamics where groups are fractious and unproductive or to a state where they are cohesive and productive. These dynamics are illustrated in Schelling's (1978) description of how segregation might occur, in spite of active efforts to intermix people of different races into residential neighborhoods.

We label the dynamics leading to a fractious and unproductive state as representing *vicious cycles* and the dynamics leading to a cohesive and productive state as representing *virtuous cycles*. These dynamics are difficult to manage unless constituting processes are explicitly identified and proactively shaped. Moreover, groups find it difficult to break the cycles that constitute these vicious and virtuous end states once they are in them.

The diversity literature has stopped short of exploring these dynamics. We argue that a process perspective is required to understand how groups characterized by diversity can create vicious or virtuous cycles. Adopting such a process perspective offers new insights on how we can manage (or not manage) diversity.

Toward a Process View of Workforce Diversity

There are many perspectives on process. One perspective examines "snapshots" at different points in time to document how an entity changes. This approach is well illustrated by diversity research that describes changes in workforce demographics over time (e.g., Bolick & Nestletroth, 1988; Johnston & Packer, 1987). The conclusion of this body of research is that diversity, once a latent possibility, is now upon us and that we must confront diversity, indeed exploit it, if we want to survive in this complex dynamic world.

Several process researchers suggest that this first perspective should be extended by identifying mechanisms that drive changes in the snapshots over time (e.g., Pettigrew, 1985; Tsoukas, 1989; Van de Ven, 1992). The basic premise here is that we might be better able to shape the evolution of an entity if we appreciate the mechanisms that drive it. In the diversity literature, for instance, globalization, competition, and proactive programs such as affirmative action have been identified as some of the mechanisms that have increased workforce diversity.

The second view on process examines interrelationships between mechanisms that drive a phenomenon (Tsoukas, 1989). These interrelationships help us understand how these mechanisms together constitute a system. That is, the whole behaves like a complex system with feedback loops and interdependencies that cannot be managed neatly. Illustrative of such a perspective is Jackson et al.'s (1995) work above.

Based upon such a systems perspective is another view of process. This view explores how vicious and virtuous cycles are created. Vicious and virtuous cycles are situations where deviations in one mechanism amplify the other successively through feedback loops. Schelling (1978) provides one such example of a deviation amplifying loop: "Hearing your car honk, I honk mine, thus encouraging you to honk yours more insistently" (p. 14).

One reason that these dynamics initiate vicious or virtuous cycles is that they are interactively complex (Perrow, 1984). That is, not only are there many mechanisms that drive the system, but these drivers are highly interrelated with one another. The presence of many drivers increases the complexity of the system, while their close relationship renders the system unstable. Small changes in one variable result in large, unanticipated, deviation-amplifying changes at the system level (Sterman, in press).

Workforce diversity dynamics have the same characteristics as the interactively complex systems that have been explored in other disciplines. There are several mechanisms that drive the dynamics of a diverse group, and these mechanisms are tightly coupled. For instance *behaviors* (exit and voice), *affect* (trust or distrust), and *perception* (of equity or inequity) are three mechanisms that interact with each other to drive diversity dynamics into vicious or virtuous states. Moreover, small deviations in any of these mechanisms can quickly drive the group to a state where members become locked into a "self-sealing" system (Kanter, 1977b, p. 249). That is, group members might find themselves locked into a set of dynamics that they are powerless to control even if they knew of its existence. Exploring how and why these vicious and virtuous cycles might arise from diversity is the key to understanding how diversity can be managed, particularly when it has the potential to polarize diverse groups and harm productivity.

In subsequent sections of this paper, we will provide a framework that can be used to explore vicious and virtuous cycles that emerge from workforce diversity. We will first identify which diversity dimension can lead to positive outcomes and which dimension can lead to negative outcomes. Based on these observations, we will offer a simple typology of groups and suggest that many contemporary groups have the dual potential of evolving toward a vicious or a virtuous state. Next, in our attempt to build a process theory of diversity, we will explore mechanisms that increase or decrease diversity in groups and therefore the outcomes of diversity. We begin with exit and voice as two manifest behavioral mechanisms that influence the outcomes of diversity. We then demonstrate how these behavioral mechanisms interact with other latent mechanisms (affect and cognition) to drive the group toward a vicious or a virtuous state.

Conceptual Framework

The conceptual framework we present here consists of three parts. In the first section, we conceptualize diversity along two dimensions: technical and institutional. In the second section, we describe the potential of voice mechanisms and exit mechanisms in increasing or decreasing the magnitude of diversity along the two dimensions. In the third section, we examine the interactions among voice, affect, and cognition mechanisms in creating vicious and virtuous cycles.

Technical and Institutional Dimensions of Diversity

To understand how groups might enhance cohesion and productivity, we must first appreciate that groups are interdependent in two arenas—the technical and the institutional (see Scott, 1987). The technical arena is one where group members are interdependent with one another on the basis of their task-related knowledge and skills (Thompson, 1967). In this arena, members focus on controlling and coordinating their technical processes to enhance the efficiency with which they as a group produce goods and services.

The institutional arena is one where group members are interdependent with one another on the basis of their work-related values. These values include the need for achievement, concern for others, honesty, and fairness (Ravlin & Meglino, 1987); they also include attitudes toward group work, risk-taking, and authority (Hofstede, 1993). The values become manifest in work rules and norms that dictate how productivity is measured, how rewards are disbursed (Scott, 1987), and how people behave on the job (England, 1967). In this arena, members focus on shaping value systems to enhance the effectiveness with which they as a group produce goods and services.

A recognition that groups are interdependent in these two arenas helps us explore which diversity dimension enhances group cohesion and productivity and which one detracts from these outcomes. For instance, a number of researchers have noted the benefits of fostering diversity of skills in the technical arena. In production systems, skill diversity allows for the specialization of tasks, thereby enhancing productivity (Simon, 1962; Taylor, 1967). In problem-solving teams, people with diverse skills can enhance creativity (Filley, House, & Kerr, 1976; Hoffman, 1979; McGrath, 1984), encourage organizational innovation (Bantel & Jackson, 1989), and create non-routine products (Gersick & Davis-Sacks, 1990). Other benefits from diversity in the technical arena stem from the flexibility that skill diversity permits (Imai,

Nonaka, & Takeuchi, 1985). Indeed, as many researchers have argued (e.g., Ashby, 1960; Morgan, 1986), internal diversity must match the external diversity of the environment. Thus, diversity of skills has the potential of creating a group where the whole is greater than the sum of its parts.

However, the realization of benefits derived from diversity of skills in the technical arena depends upon the similarity of work-related values in the institutional arena. A similarity of work-related values in the institutional arena creates an opportunity for the institution of common rules, norms, and beliefs that form the basis for stable expectations required for group cohesion and productivity. Indeed, similarity of values fosters common objectives, group identity, acceptance of member roles, and a set of shared understandings concerning individual and group performance (Carron, 1986; Fulkerson & Schuler, 1992; McClure & Foster, 1991). However, to the extent that these work-related values are different and in conflict with one another, misunderstandings and conflicts inevitably arise as a result of dissimilar expectations.

Thus, once we begin exploring the impact of diversity in the technical and institutional arenas on group cohesion and productivity, we see two different outcomes: Diversity in the technical arena has the potential for yielding positive outcomes; and diversity in the institutional arena has the potential for yielding negative outcomes. For a group to be cohesive and productive, therefore, diversity of skills in the technical arena must be matched with similarity of work-related values in the institutional arena. More formally stated:

> *Proposition 1:* A group is more likely to be cohesive and productive to the extent that group members have diverse task-related skills and similar work-related values.

Several conceptual and empirical pieces of work lend support to this basic proposition. For instance, Olson (1969) suggested that groups are more likely to be cohesive and productive if "People are socialized to have diverse wants with respect to private goods [skills] and similar wants with respect to collective goods [values]" (p. 151). Jackson et al. (1995) observed that tolerance for task-based conflicts in decision-making teams may be present when team members are homogeneous in terms of some non-task attributes. At the organizational level of analysis, this view is substantiated by Lawrence and Lorsch (1967) who demonstrated that differentiation and integration together have the potential to yield more favorable organizational outcomes.

Once stated, *Proposition 1* above seems obvious—almost a truism. However, in practice, we find it very difficult to create groups that are likely to be cohesive and productive. This difficulty arises in part because of an inherent tension in the formation of many groups in contemporary environments, where efforts to benefit from diversity in the technical arena automatically lead to diversity in the institutional arena. For instance, to access diverse skills, temporary groups may be formed by bringing together people from different departments, organizations, or countries. These groups are typically used in organizations with quality circles, special task forces, or problem-solving teams. The formation of such groups increases diversity in the institutional arena as group members bring in different work-related values. Indeed, these types of temporary groups are becoming very common, with increasing pressures to develop new products rapidly, threat of overseas competition, and demand for quality.

Such a diverse group has the potential for being either cohesive and productive or fractious and unproductive. Diverse skills, when brought together in some meaningful way, can generate positive outcomes. However, as we stated earlier, conflicting values render it difficult for group members to meaningfully integrate their diverse skills. Team members may end up working at odds with one another without a common purpose, leading to a situation where the whole is less than the sum of its parts.

We label a group characterized by diversity in both technical and institutional arenas as an *uneasy alliance*, as it has the potential for evolving to a state where the group is cohesive and productive or to a state where the group is fractious and unproductive as seen in quadrant 1 of Figure 1. This figure also depicts three other types of groups. Consistent with *Proposition 1*, quadrant 2 represents a group that is cohesive and productive at the skill level, with little diversity of values. We label such a group as an *easy alliance*. Quadrant 3 represents a group characterized by lack of diversity in both technical and institutional arenas. We label such a group as an *unproductive alliance*. In this type of group, similarity of skills in the technical arena may at best reduce productivity (as there is no division of labor), and at worst, may lead to conflict over a common pool of resources.

Despite such an unproductive arrangement in the technical arena, group members might still be cohesive because they have similar work-related values in the institutional arena. A hypothetical example of such an unproductive arrangement is a group of male salesmen with similar ethnic backgrounds, each possessing very similar skills and earning sales commissions from a common pool of resources. Quadrant 4 represents a group characterized by similarity of skills and diversity of values. We label such a group as a *fractious alliance*. Conflict created by similar skills in the technical arena is often confounded by diversity of values in the institutional arena, which results in the absence of a common language, trust, and beliefs. Illustrative of this situation is conflict arising between people with vastly different value systems with regard to work norms, communication styles, attitudes, and beliefs.

Figure 1: Determinants of Group Cohesion and Productivity

		No (DIVERSE VALUES)	Yes (DIVERSE VALUES)
DIVERSE SKILLS	Yes	*QUADRANT 2* Easy Alliance	*QUADRANT 1* Uneasy Alliance
	No	*QUADRANT 3* Unproductive Alliance	*QUADRANT 4* Fractious Alliance

DIVERSE VALUES

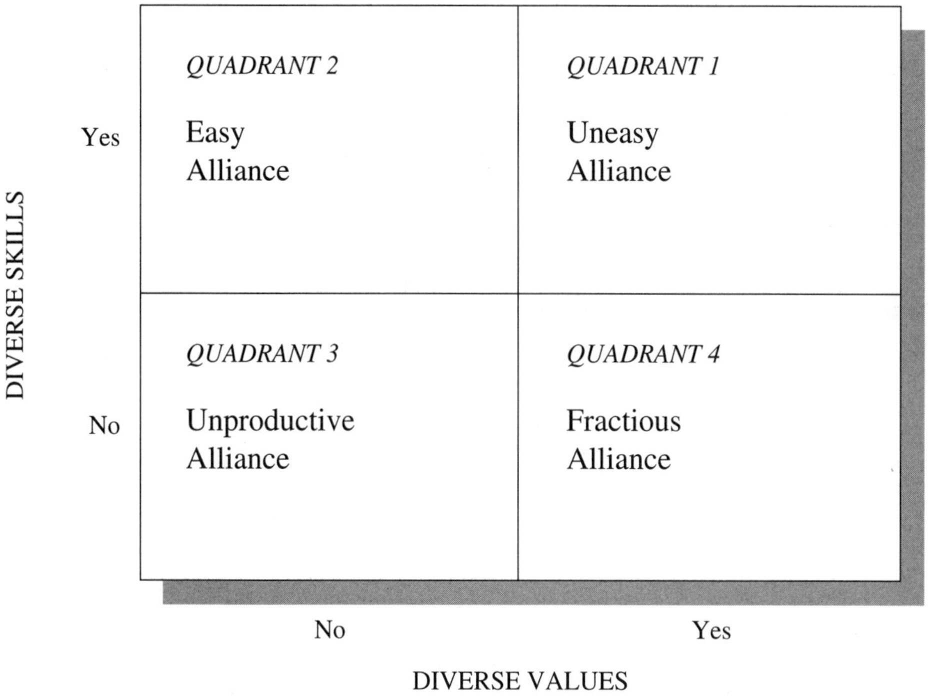

As we mentioned earlier, many groups may be characterized as being in an uneasy alliance; therefore, they are of particular interest to us here. As these groups have the dual potential of evolving toward a virtuous or a vicious cycle, a key question is: Which quadrant will a group in an uneasy alliance gravitate toward over time? To answer this question, we must develop an appreciation of the processes by which groups form, change, and dissipate. That is, not only must we gain an appreciation of what is conducive for cohesion and productivity but also an appreciation of how group cohesion and productivity evolve over time through group interactions.

There are clearly some boundaries and limitations to the theory that we offer here. First, our focus is on self-managed work teams (those that form and disband voluntarily with no supervision). We do not explore the dynamics that might unfold in other types of groups. Second, we focus on those groups that may be characterized as being in a state of uneasy alliance. Groups starting from a different quadrant in Figure 1 may exhibit different dynamics because of their initial starting conditions; we do not explore these issues in this paper. Third, in developing our theory, we focus on work-related values and not on larger cultural differences. However, we submit that our arguments could potentially be extended to the effect of cultural differences on work group cohesion and productivity.

Diversity Drivers

The basic elements of our framework used to explore the dynamics that emerge from diversity are outlined in Figure 2.

Most researchers suggest that a process perspective requires an appreciation of the mechanisms that shape the evolution of an entity over time (e.g., Pettigrew, 1985; Tsoukas, 1989; Van de Ven, 1992). This statement, when applied to our framework (Figure 1), suggests that mechanisms such as behaviors, affect, and cognition that increase or decrease the level of diversity in the technical and institutional arenas will drive a group in an uneasy alliance to one or the other quadrants depending upon which diversity dimension is amplified or decreased. For instance, in the institutional arena, mechanisms that decrease the diversity of values have the potential of driving an uneasy alliance toward an easy alliance. In the instrumental arena, mechanisms that increase the similarity of skills have the potential of driving an uneasy alliance toward a fractious alliance. Operating together, these mechanisms have the potential of driving an uneasy alliance toward an unproductive alliance. Stated in the form of an extension to *Proposition 1:*

> *Proposition 2:* Mechanisms that maintain or increase diversity
> of skills and those that bridge or decrease diversity of values
> will render a group more cohesive and productive.

Voice mechanisms. Voice is one of the behavioral mechanisms that affects the outcomes of diversity (Hirschman, 1970). Voice mechanisms, such as regularly scheduled meetings and other forums for communication, provide people the opportunity to express concerns, raise problems, seek clarification, and provide solutions. Consequently, these mechanisms help people

Figure 2: Process Model of Group Diversity

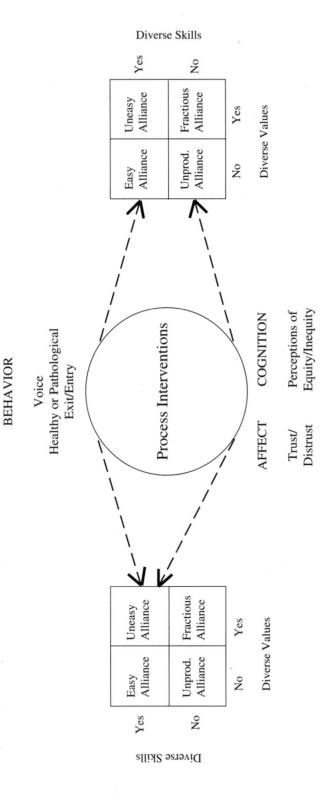

learn about differences that exist between groups and reduce the possibility of group members negatively viewing differences in values. As Jackson (1992) suggests, voice mechanisms can be used to surface issues, exchange points of view, and discuss possible alternatives for resolving differences that might threaten the ability of people to work together effectively. Lacking effective voice mechanisms, differences in values have the potential of creating different perceptions about phenomena, negative views about out-groups, and conflict between group members.

Several companies have successfully used appropriate voice mechanisms to manage diversity. For instance, at Digital Equipment Corporation, employees defuse misunderstandings due to differences in values across departments through small-group dialogue (Walker & Hanson, 1992, p. 120). Other corporations, like Xerox and PepsiCo, have found that encouraging group dialogue through caucus groups enhances employee involvement in their efforts to manage workforce diversity (Fulkerson & Schuler, 1992; Sessa, 1992). Voice mechanisms essentially help in creating common ground and common bonds among diverse employees (Gottfredson, 1992).

Exit mechanism. Exit (or entry) is a second mechanism that affects the outcomes of diversity (Hirschman, 1970; Olson, 1969). Olson (1969) pointed out that a group will more likely regenerate itself by continually changing the constitution of its members, a process known as *churning*. By doing this, groups can acquire and divest skills as required, thereby creating a process that is conducive to learning and group regeneration.

Indeed, such a churning of skills is the hallmark of many temporary teams that include product development and top-management teams. Chaganti and Sambharya (1987) found that organizations competing on the basis of new product development tend to have a large proportion of outsiders in their upper echelons. Churning has been found to have beneficial effects on top-management responsiveness to environmental shock (Murmann & Tushman, 1994). Finkelstein and Hambrick (1990) found that teams, where top managers had short tenures, pursued novel strategies. In contrast, teams, where top managers had long tenures, experienced negative outcomes including escalation of commitment, risk aversion, and restriction on information processing.

Challenges in managing voice and exit. Actions that encourage voice and exit are important for group cohesion and productivity. However, there are two challenges in managing a group with these behavioral mechanisms. First, excessive voice and exit can be deleterious for group cohesion and productivity. In excess, voice overloads a communication system, thereby reducing its power to act as a means to bridge diverse value systems. Moreover, excessive voice might detract from a group's ability to accomplish its tasks in the technical arena. Similarly, excessive exit or entry can prevent a group from developing a stable, shared value system in the institutional arena.

The second challenge in managing a diverse group becomes apparent in our discussion above, pertaining to the negative impact of exit and entry behaviors on value stability, and their positive impact on the reconstitution of skills. It suggests that the very mechanisms that affect diversity in one arena can also affect diversity in the other (see Olson, 1969, for a detailed discussion of this point). In particular, exit and entry, while maintaining and enhancing the diversity of skills in the technical arena, also result in enhancing diversity of values in the institutional arena.

Just as exit and entry can simultaneously lead to positive and negative outcomes in the two different arenas, so too can voice. Specifically, while voice mechanisms provide members an opportunity to learn about each other's value systems, they can also reduce the diversity of skills in the technical arena through mimetic learning, that is vicarious learning or observation and emulation (DiMaggio & Powell, 1983; Miller, 1990; Van de Ven & Walker, 1984). Regenerating skills through churning, therefore, might appear to be an attractive alternative. However, as we have already pointed out, churning itself increases diversity of values in the institutional arena, thereby destabilizing the group.

These trade-offs can be managed by choosing the level of productivity and value stability required for each project and by building in practices to compensate for the unintended consequences of voice and entry. For instance, programmed tasks that require regularity might be accomplished by groups where there is not much entry and where members have been socialized to have similar values. Fine-tuning of skills can be accomplished through training programs. In contrast, non-programmed tasks that are changing continually may be accomplished by fostering periodic entry and exit of group members. Potential disruptions that entrants may create in the institutional arena may be reduced by instituting programs to socialize newcomers.

Interactions that Create Vicious and Virtuous Cycles

Although these trade-offs can be managed, true challenges from diversity arise from our inability to manage more complex interdependencies between behaviors, such as voice and exit and other latent mechanisms that drive diversity dynamics. In combination with these latent drivers, the presence or absence of voice or exit can lead to a virtuous or a vicious cycle.

The diversity literature reveals two such latent mechanisms—cognition and affect (Kanter, 1977a; Triandis, Hall, & Ewen, 1965). Diverse perspectives that emanate from different value systems can give rise to misunderstandings and conflict. Similarly, feelings of trust and distrust are central to group cohesion and productivity, which in turn are related to the behaviors of exit and voice. Together, cognition, affect, and behaviors create a complex system that has the potential of evolving toward a vicious or virtuous cycle.

To understand the constitution of these dynamics, consider a group where voice mechanisms have not been established. As we noted earlier, different value systems foster different perceptions about how group events are interpreted, how relationships are valued, and how inputs and rewards are measured. When confronted with such a situation, the absence of appropriate voice mechanisms prevents members from clarifying their inputs and rewards. Consequently, the absence of voice mechanisms can result in fostering a sense of inequity among group members.

To the extent that exit is also not possible, perceptions of inequity will lead to a reduction of work inputs. We label such an outcome as *partial exit*; that is, members are physically present but reduce their contributions. Partial exit enhances perceptions of inequity and a sense that some might be getting a free ride through the efforts of others. Such a cycle is all the more possible in the absence of voice.

Perceptions that group members might be getting a free ride, along with an inability to voice concerns and clarify issues, can also foster a feeling in the group that their peers are behaving opportunistically. This feeling can be amplified at early stages of group formation when stable expectations for behavior and interactions have yet to be established. Under these conditions, members with different skills and values might develop diverse expectations and psychological contracts (Rousseau & Parks, 1992), that when seemingly abrogated, enhance feelings of distrust.

Distrust and perception of inequity can polarize group members into in-groups and out-groups, within their own subcultures. Such polarization can destroy whatever meaningful voice there is between subgroups. Polarization also results in partial exit as members reduce contributions to the group while pursuing subgoals. In this way the loop is closed, thereby creating a set of dynamics that is detrimental to group cohesion and productivity.

This discussion only illustrates the type of dynamics that group members might experience in their interactions as they stumble into a vicious cycle. As process researchers have noted (e.g., Mohr, 1982), there are several different ways by which end states can be reached. Consequently, in articulating dynamics that lead a group to a vicious end state, we can only be illustrative and leave the particulars to the vagaries of the processes that unfold within each group.

It is for this reason that we are reluctant to state the specific relationships between the driving mechanisms (behavior, affect, and cognition) in the form of a proposition. However, our discussion does suggest that the absence of voice and exit can increase the likelihood of initiating a vicious cycle.

Proposition 3: Absence of voice and exit mechanisms increases the likelihood of initiating a vicious cycle.

What initiates a divergence of perceptions? Culbert (1970) argues that group members must first explore what integrates them before they can be comfortable exploring what divides them. In other words, group members are more likely to perceive their differences to be a threat if their interactions are initially anchored on differences in value systems rather than differences in skills. In the absence of voice, a vicious cycle is more likely to be initiated if a group initially directs its attention on value differences in the institutional arena, while ignoring the benefits of their interdependence in the technical arena.

Proposition 4: A vicious cycle is more likely to be initiated if a group's interactions are initially anchored on differences in value systems rather than differences in skills.

In contrast, group members are more likely to see the benefits of collaborating with one another if their interactions are anchored on diversity in the technical arena. A recognition of the benefits of collaborating with one another creates a context in which members can institute voice mechanisms that allow them to explore differences and create similarities in the institutional arena. Moreover, voice helps members develop a sense of the worth of their own skills in relation to those offered by others and the whole. Such an appreciation alleviates feelings of inequity that arise when experts from different professions come together. Moreover, the goodwill that prevails during these initial stages, in combination with a recognition of the benefits of interacting with others possessing diverse skills, can create an environment where distrust, while being latent, is muted. To the extent that exit is possible, if voice fails, disgruntled members leave the group, thereby reducing partial exit. Thus the presence of voice and exit mechanisms increases the likelihood of initiating a virtuous cycle.

In sum, the presence or absence of mechanisms that encourage voice, exit, and entry, and the locus of initial interactions (i.e., whether or not a group's focus is on diversity in the technical or the institutional arena) have an important bearing on whether a vicious or a virtuous cycle is initiated. These observations are summarized in Figure 3.

Discussion and Implications

Our discussion on workforce diversity began with two questions: Which facets of diversity lead to cohesion and productivity? and, What are the dynamics that unfold from diversity? Our subsequent discussion reflects the complexity surrounding workforce diversity dynamics, wherein several mechanisms interactively drive groups in different directions. Indeed, this interactive complexity creates a system where groups might unintentionally initiate vicious or virtuous cycles.

Exploring these cycles, Masuch (1985) noted: "Vicious cycles lead an absurd existence since everyone should avoid deviation-amplifying feedback. Yet, once caught in a vicious cycle, human actors continue on a path of action that leads further and further away from the desired state of affairs" (pp. 22-23). Similarly, referring to such vicious cycles, Kanter (1977b) observed: "It is hard for a person to break out of the cycle once begun" and that these "self-perpetuating, self-sealing systems . . . can be broken only from [the] outside" (p. 249). It is for this reason that external intervention is required to break a vicious cycle.

Interventions

Although external intervention is required to break a vicious cycle, managers frequently intervene with solutions that exacerbate the problem they are supposed to alleviate. This is because these interventions essentially are one-shot attempts to adjudicate between group disputes and to impose solutions—what we label as *variance interventions*. These are interventions that dictate end outcomes to be accomplished without specifying the means by which such outcomes might be realized. In contrast, *process interventions* are attempts to shape the unfolding dynamics by influencing the underlying forces that drive the process. In other words, process interventionists appreciate that sometimes the means to accomplish end outcomes are as important, if

Figure 3. Vicious and Virtuous Facets of Diversity

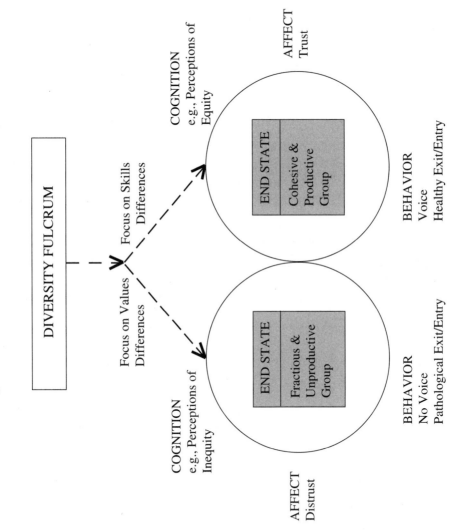

not more so, as the outcomes themselves. Often, those caught up in a vicious cycle are unable to identify and implement the means to change their end outcomes.

Weick (1979) offers one perspective as to why managers frequently intervene with variance solutions to solve a process problem. He stated: "Most managers get into trouble because they forget to think in circles. Managerial problems persist because managers continue to believe that there are such things as unilateral causation, independent and dependent variables, origins, and terminations" (p. 86). Indeed, this variance problem is exacerbated in the context of diversity, a term that seduces us to think in variance terms. In its rawest form, diversity is manifest primarily in the form of statistics that are most amenable to capture similarities and dissimilarities that we look for. Yet the outcomes of interactions between heterogeneous people only emerge through complex processes.

Affirmative action illustrates a variance intervention used to address a process problem, viewed in the form of statistical imbalances in the workforce. Affirmative action in hiring or, at best, in promotions provides opportunity for entry but little else. Managers institute an affirmative action program and then await its results (Thomas, 1992). The reason that such initiatives come undone, according to Thomas, is that affirmative action programs are artificial, whereas challenges from diversity require continuous attention and effort. To handle the vicious cycle of statistical imbalances, managerial interventions must be processual. By this we mean process tools are necessary for addressing the challenges groups might encounter as group dynamics unfold. Accordingly, attention to managing diversity requires opportunities for training and skill development and for growth and experience that will position a minority member on the fast track. These changes are not possible without a change in the attitude of people and the promotion of a culture that appreciates diversity. In their current form, interventions such as affirmative action programs can lead to a perception of reverse discrimination, fueling the vicious cycle between inequity, distrust, and conflictual behavior.

Weick (1979) provides an example of a process intervention that can be used to break a vicious cycle once it has already taken hold. Recognizing that vicious cycles are created by the presence of a number of variables interacting closely with one another (a facet that Perrow [1984] labels as representing interactive complexity), Weick suggests that these variables should be decoupled. By doing this, the interactive complexity that creates vicious cycles is alleviated, rendering the system more manageable. For instance,

Walker and Hanson (1992) provide an illustration of how tightly coupled drivers that constitute a vicious cycle can be decoupled. They describe how Digital Equipment Corporation employees were better able to exercise voice and agree to an overarching set of values by decoupling affect and perceptions (p. 124).

Walker and Hanson describe how the managers at Digital, at hearing themselves described as racist and sexist, at first thought they were being accused of being bad people. Hence, they would become defensive and shut down. The women and minority participants, in turn, would at times become enraged and engage in behavior that appeared irrational. Whenever the two sides came close to discussing critical issues, communication would invariably break down. As a result, there was little opportunity for learning on either side. Following intervention, managers became less defensive as they came to understand they were not being accused of being bad people and were able to talk openly about the issues of race and the stereotypes they held about blacks and women.

Managers can provide process tools for work groups to help them avoid vicious cycles. These tools include an appreciation of the various types of voice mechanisms, avoidance of unequal or too much voice, and an understanding of how the group might deal with conflict and pathological exit. Process tools also include training programs that help regenerate skills in the technical arena. Programs can be designed to sensitize people to differences between their own and others' value systems, and to the ways in which these differences affect cognition, affect, and behaviors (Albert, 1986; Triandis, 1984).

Gersick's (1988) work suggests when these process interventions might have the greatest impact on group dynamics. In her study of eight naturally forming groups, she found that there appear to be two critical periods when groups are most open to external influence. The first is the initial meeting when group interactions set lasting precedents that hold special potential to influence a team's basic approach toward its project. During this period, external intervention can direct group members' attention to benefits from diversity in the technical arena, while providing them with the process tools to deal with the challenges associated with diversity in the institutional arena.

Gersick (1988) found a second opportunity for effective external intervention. Not only did teams open up to outside influence at a point midway through their interactions—they actively used outside resources as a basis for recharting the course of their work. This midpoint, for us, would be soon after adolescence, when once the liabilities have been overcome, external intervention might help the group articulate a common value system that binds their future task activities.

Implications for Research

To conduct research that explores processual aspects of diversity, we recommend a design that is inductive and flexible, in order to benefit from the learning that occurs through observation. Our model and its associated vocabulary are only valuable in initiating the research. We recommend such a research design because process research must be able to capture dynamics as they unfold. As data on several groups are accumulated, theory must be shaped even as it is tested provisionally—a process that Glaser and Strauss (1967) label as *analytic induction* (see also Platt's [1964] work on strong inference). Over time, as evidence on different groups accumulates, it will be possible to tease out differences in dynamics that distinguish groups that are cohesive and productive from those that are fractious and unproductive.

This research design implies the following concrete steps. First, it is important to adopt a longitudinal approach. Following Poole's (1983) work, the researcher should be able to track mechanisms that increase or decrease diversity in the technical and institutional arenas and examine the effect of these changes on cohesion and productivity. Second, the researcher needs to examine whether the developmental patterns that constitute virtuous cycles differ from those that constitute vicious cycles. To accomplish this objective, the researcher needs to track the constructs that we have offered in this paper. These constructs include the presence or absence (and type) of voice and exit. Tracking affect and cognition will require periodic self-reports from group members based on a questionnaire given to them. Such a questionnaire, by its very nature, will be obtrusive as it will serve to sensitize group members to certain issues.

The most obtrusive approach will be to engage in action science (Argyris, Putnam, & Smith, 1985). This is an approach that is essential for understanding the effect of managerial intervention on diversity dynamics. We maintain that process interventions are required to address process problems, and that variance interventions might exacerbate the very problems that they are designed to alleviate. Action-science research will be able to address this.

Conclusion

The metaphor of the melting pot has frequently been used to evoke positive images about environments that foster diversity. However, implicit in the use of this metaphor is an inadequate appreciation of the vicious facets associated with diversity when one group tries to assimilate another. As Kilborn (1990) suggests, assimilation represents the domination of one culture over others, not the melding of many. Indeed, this very assimilation process can polarize different social groups and harm productivity, thereby detracting from a group's ability to harness the benefits from diversity (Gottfredson, 1992).

Recognizing this weakness in the melting pot metaphor, Gottfredson (1992) suggests a salad as a metaphor that captures both the benefits and challenges of diversity. The salad, as a metaphor, is more appropriate than the melting pot because a salad preserves the diversity and integrity of its ingredients. At the same time, the appeal of a salad is enhanced or diminished by how it is mixed. It is precisely this processual aspect that lends diversity its allure. Whether or not a group benefits from diversity depends upon the processes that unfold.

References

Albert, R. D. (1986). Conceptual framework for the development and the evaluation of cross-cultural orientation programs. *International Journal of Inter-cultural Relations, 10,* 197-213.

Argyris, C., Putnam, R., & Smith, D. M. (1985). *Action science.* San Francisco: Jossey-Bass.

Ashby, W. R. (1960). *Design for a brain.* New York: John Wiley.

Bantel, K. A., & Jackson, S. E. (1989). Top management and innovations in banking: Does the composition of the top team make a difference? *Strategic Management Journal, 10,* 107-124.

Bolick, C., & Nestletroth, S. (1988). *Opportunity 2000: Creating affirmative action strategies for a changing workforce.* Washington, DC: U.S. Government Printing Office.

Brislin, R. W. (1981). *Cross-cultural encounters: Face-to-face encounters.* New York: Pergamon.

Carron, A. V. (1986). The sport team as an effective group. In J. Williams (Ed.), *Applied sport psychology, personal growth to peak performance* (pp. 75-91). Palo Alto, CA: Mayfield.

Chaganti, R., & Sambharya, R. (1987). Strategic orientation and characteristics of upper management. *Strategic Management Journal, 8,* 393-401.

Culbert, S. (1970). Accelerating laboratory learning through a phase regression mode; for trainer intervention. *Journal of Applied Behavioral Science, 6,* 21-38.

DiMaggio, P., & Powell, W. (1983). The iron cage revisited: Institutional and collective rationality in organizational fields. *American Sociological Review, 48,* 147-160.

England, G. W. (1967). Organizational goals and expected behavior of American managers. *Academy of Management Journal, 10,* 107-117.

Ferdman, B. M. (1992). The dynamics of ethnic diversity in organizations: Toward integrative models. In K. Kelly (Ed.), *Issues, theory and research in industrial/ organizational psychology* (pp. 339-384). Amsterdam, The Netherlands: North-Holland.

Filley, A. C., House, R. J., & Kerr, S. (1976). *Managerial process and organizational behavior.* Glenview, IL: Scott Foresman.

Finkelstein, S., & Hambrick, D. C. (1990). Top management tenure and organizational outcomes: The moderating role of managerial discretion. *Administrative Science Quarterly, 35,* 485-503.

Friedman, M., & Friedman, R. (1980). *Free to choose.* New York: Harcourt-Brace.

Fulkerson, J. R., & Schuler, R. S. (1992). Managing worldwide diversity at Pepsi-Cola International. In S. E. Jackson & Associates (Eds.), *Diversity in the workplace: Human resources initiatives* (pp. 248-278). New York: Guilford Press.

Gersick, C. J. (1988). Time and transition in work teams: Toward a new model of group development. *Academy of Management Journal, 31,* 9-14.

Gersick, C. J., & Davis-Sacks, M. L. (1990). Summary: Task forces. In J. R. Hackman (Ed.), *Groups that work (and those that don't work)* (pp. 146-153). San Francisco: Jossey-Bass.

Glaser, B. G., & Strauss, A. L. (1967). *The discovery of grounded theory: Strategies for qualitative research.* Chicago: Aldine.

Gottfredson, L. S. (1992). Dilemmas in developing diversity programs. In S. E. Jackson & Associates (Eds.), *Diversity in the workplace: Human resources initiatives* (pp. 279-305). New York: Guilford Press.

Hirschman, A. O. (1970). *Exit, voice and loyalty: Responses to decline in firms, organizations, and states.* Cambridge, MA: Harvard University Press.

Hoffman, L. R. (1979). Applying experimental research on group problem solving to organizations. *Journal of Applied Behavioral Science, 15,* 375-391.

Hofstede, G. (1983). National cultures in four dimensions. *International Studies of Management and Organization, 13,* 46-74.

Imai, K., Nonaka, I., & Takeuchi, H. (1985). Managing the new product development process: How Japanese companies learn and unlearn. In K. B. Clark, R. Hayes, & C. Lorenz (Eds.), *The uneasy alliance: Managing the productivity technology dilemma* (pp. 337-376). Cambridge, MA: Harvard Business School Press.

Jackson, S. E. (1992). Stepping into the future: Guidelines for action. In S. E. Jackson & Associates (Eds.), *Diversity in the workplace: Human resources initiatives* (pp. 319-339). New York: Guilford Press.

Jackson, S. E., & Alvarez, E. B. (1992). Working through diversity as a strategic imperative. In S. E. Jackson & Associates (Eds.), *Diversity in the workplace: Human resources initiatives* (pp. 13-29). New York: Guilford Press.

Jackson, S. E., Brett, J. F., Sessa, V. I., Cooper, D. M., Julin, J. A., & Peyronnin, K. (1991). Some differences make a difference: Individual dissimilarity and group heterogeneity as correlates of recruitment, promotions and turnover. *Journal of Applied Psychology, 76,* 675-689.

Jackson, S. E., May, K. E., & Whitney, K. (1995). Understanding the dynamics of diversity in decision making teams. In R. A. Guzzo & E. Salas (Eds.), *Team effectiveness and decision making in organizations.* San Francisco: Jossey-Bass.

Jackson, S. E., Stone, V. K., & Alvarez, E. B. (1993). Socialization amidst diversity: Impact of demographics on work team old-timers and newcomers. In L. L. Cummings & B. M. Staw (Eds.), *Research in organizational behavior* (Vol. 15, pp. 45-109). Greenwich, CT: JAI Press.

Johnston, W. B., & Packer, A. H. (1987). *Workforce 2000: Work and workers for the 21st century.* Indianapolis: Hudson Institute.

Kanter, R. M. (1977a). Some effects of proportions on group life: Skewed sex ratios and responses to token women. *American Journal of Sociology, 82,* 965-990.

Kanter, R. M. (1977b). *Men and women of the corporation.* New York: Basic Books.

Kilborn, P. T. (1990, October 4). A company recasts itself to erase decades of bias. *New York Times,* pp. A1, D21.

Lawrence, P. R., & Lorsch, J. W. (1967). *Organization and environment.* Boston: Harvard University Press.

Masuch, M. (1985). Vicious circles in organizations. *Administrative Science Quarterly, 30,* 14-33.

McClure, B. A., & Foster, C. D. (1991). Group work as a method of promoting cohesiveness within a women's gymnastics team. *Perceptual and Motor Skills, 73,* 307-313.

McGrath, J. E. (1984). *Groups: Interaction and performance.* Englewood Cliffs, NJ: Prentice Hall.

Miller, D. (1990). *The Icarus paradox: How exceptional companies bring about their own downfall.* New York: Harper Business.

Mohr, L. B. (1982). *Explaining organizational behavior: The limits and possibilities of theory and research.* San Francisco: Jossey-Bass.

Morgan, G. (1986). *Images of organization.* Beverly Hills, CA: Sage.

Murrman, P., & Tushman, M. L. (1994). Impacts of executive team characteristics and organizational context on organization responsiveness to environmental shock. *NYU Conference on Technological Oversights and Foresights,* New York, NY.

Olson, M., Jr. (1969). The relationship between economics and other social sciences: The province of a social report. In S. M. Lipset (Ed.), *Politics and the social sciences* (pp. 137-162). New York: Oxford University Press.

O'Reilly, C. A., Caldwell, D. F., & Barnett, W. P. (1989). Work group demography, social integration, and turnover. *Administrative Science Quarterly, 34,* 21-37.

Perrow, C. (1984). *Normal accidents: Living with high-risk technologies.* New York: Basic Books.

Pettigrew, A. (1985). *The awakening giant: Continuity and change in ICI.* New York: Basil Blackwell Ltd.

Platt, J. R. (1964). Strong inference. *Science, 146*(3642), 347-353.

Poole, M. S. (1983). Decision development in small groups II: A study of multiple sequence of decision making. *Communication Monographs, 50,* 206-232.

Ravlin, E. C., & Meglino, B. M. (1987). Effects of values on perception and decision making: A study of alternative work value measures. *Journal of Applied Psychology, 72,* 666-673.

Rousseau, D. M., & Parks, J. (1992). The contracts of individuals and organizations. In L. L. Cummings & B. M. Staw (Eds.), *Research in organizational behavior* (Vol. 15, pp. 1-47). Greenwich, CT: JAI Press.

Schelling, T. C. (1978). *Micromotives and macrobehavior.* New York: Norton.

Scott, W. R. (1987). *Organizations: Rational, natural and open systems* (2nd ed.). Englewood Cliffs, NJ: Prentice Hall.

Sessa, V. I. (1992). Managing diversity at Xerox Corporation: Balanced workforce goals and caucus groups. In S. E. Jackson & Associates (Eds.), *Diversity in the workplace: Human resources initiatives* (pp. 37-64). New York: Guilford Press.

Simon, H. A. (1962). The architecture of complexity. *Proceedings of the American Philosophical Society, 106,* 476-482.

Sterman, J. D. (in press). Learning in and about complex systems. *Systems Dynamics Review.*

Taylor, F. W. (1967). *Principles of scientific management.* New York: Norton.

Thomas, R. R., Jr. (1992). Managing diversity: A conceptual framework. In S. E. Jackson & Associates (Eds.), *Diversity in the workplace: Human resources initiatives* (pp. 306-308). New York: Guilford Press.

Thompson, J. D. (1967). *Organizations in action.* New York: McGraw-Hill.

Triandis, H. C. (1984). A theoretical framework for the more efficient construction of culture assimilators. *International Journal of Inter-cultural Relations, 8,* 301-330.

Triandis, H. C., Hall, E. R., & Ewen, R. B. (1965). Member heterogeneity and dyadic creativity. *Human Relations, 18,* 33-56.

Tsoukas, H. (1989). The validity of idiographic research explanations. *Academy of Management Review, 14,* 551-561.

Tsui, A. S., & O'Reilly, C. A., III (1989). Beyond simple demographic effects: The importance of relational demography in superior-subordinate dyads. *Academy of Management Journal, 32,* 402-423.

Van de Ven, A. H. (1992). Suggestions for studying strategy process: A research note. *Strategic Management Journal, 13,* 169-188.

Van de Ven, A. H., & Walker, G. (1984). Dynamics of interorganizational coordination. *Administrative Science Quarterly, 29,* 598-621.

Wagner, W. G., Pfeffer, J., & O'Reilly, C. A., III (1984). Organizational demography and turnover in top-management groups. *Administrative Science Quarterly, 29,* 74-92.

Walker, B. A., & Hanson, W. C. (1992). Valuing differences at Digital Equipment Corporation. In S. E. Jackson & Associates (Eds.), *Diversity in the workplace: Human resources initiatives* (pp. 119-137). New York: Guilford Press.

Weick, K. E. (1979). *The social psychology of organizing* (2nd ed.). New York: Random House.

Directions for Further Research

Marian N. Ruderman
Martha W. Hughes-James
Susan E. Jackson

The papers in this book add to a small but growing field of research on diverse teams. They contribute to the literature by providing systematic ways of looking at the dynamics of diversity in the context of work teams. When we issued the call for papers, we hoped to locate studies that would identify the causes and processes that explain and predict the benefits and liabilities of diversity within work teams. What we found were studies that demonstrated small, and usually dysfunctional, effects of diversity. Evidence of the benefits of diversity appears to be scarce.

One explanation for the lack of positive consequences associated with diversity is that the field studies were carried out in organizations in which diversity was not actively managed. None of the organizations studied prepared their teams to deal with their own diversity. The teams studied often were functioning in the context of a single dominant culture, receiving little support for accessing the diverse perspectives of members. It takes more than simply putting a diverse group together to realize the benefits of diversity (Cox, 1993). Future research needs to take differences in organizational support for diversity into account.

A related area for further research is to look at interventions for reducing the feelings of discomfort associated with diversity. Progress has been made in the laboratory in this regard (Brewer, 1995) and there are examples of successful interventions from the field (Armstrong & Cole, 1995; Katz & Miller, 1993). Nevertheless, we have little systematic knowledge about the principles of successful intervention. Additional research in organizational settings is necessary to understand how to reduce these dysfunctional reactions to diversity. Toward this end, Raghuram and Garud suggest mechanisms that might be of use in enhancing group process in diverse groups.

Some of the papers in this book provide guidance for the leaders of diverse teams. The work of James, Chen, and Cropanzano; Mayo, Meindl, and Pastor; and Gelfand, Kuhn, and Radhakrishnan suggests that looking at diverse teams from the leader's perspective is a fruitful area for research. These papers further suggest that managers can do well by taking the values of their direct reports into account when communicating and designing organizational structures and systems. More research on leaders is sorely needed in order to help managers realize the potential of diverse groups.

Finally, we hope that future research will improve our understanding of the consequences of diversity across extended periods of time and in differing contexts. With the exception of the work by Kossek, Zonia, and Young, the field studies reported in this volume used cross-sectional research designs. The results of DiTomaso, Cordero, and Farris and the process explanation offered by Raghuram and Garud suggest that studies of how groups evolve over time may provide new insights. In terms of context, we need more research to improve our understanding of how organizational cultures, management processes, and team structures interact with the diversity present in a team to shape the evolution of its internal dynamics and the reactions of individual members.

References

Armstrong, D. J., & Cole, P. (1995). Managing distances and differences in geographically distributed work groups. In S. E. Jackson & M. N. Ruderman (Eds.), *Diversity in work teams: Research paradigms for a changing workplace*. Washington, DC: American Psychological Association.

Brewer, M. B. (1995). Managing diversity: Can we reap the benefits without paying the costs? In S. E. Jackson & M. N. Ruderman (Eds.), *Diversity in work teams: Research paradigms for a changing workplace*. Washington, DC: American Psychological Association.

Cox, T. H. (1993). *Cultural diversity in organizations: Theory, research, and practice.* San Francisco: Berrett-Koehler.

Katz, J. H., & Miller, F. A. (1993). High performance and inclusion: A new model for teams. *The Diversity Factor, 2*(1), 2-7.

Biographical Sketches of Contributors

Dz-Lyang Chen has his own consulting firm, East-West Management Consulting, Inc., in Taiwan. He is a contract representative of Personnel Decisions, Inc. for Asia and has been a lecturer at the National University of Taiwan. He has a Ph.D. in organizational psychology from Colorado State University.

Rene Cordero is an assistant professor in the Department of Management, School of Industrial Administration, New Jersey Institute of Technology, Newark, New Jersey. He specializes in the management of technology. Cordero has a Ph.D. from Rutgers, the State University of New Jersey.

Russell Cropanzano is associate professor of industrial/organizational psychology at Colorado State University. His principal research interest concerns perceptions of workplace justice. Cropanzano received his Ph.D. from Purdue University.

Nancy DiTomaso is a professor and chair of the Department of Organization Management at Rutgers Faculty of Management. She specializes in the management of diversity and change in organizations. DiTomaso holds a Ph.D. from the University of Wisconsin, Madison.

Keith M. Eigel is a doctoral student in psychology at the University of Georgia. His research interests are team composition, team process, and leadership development at both the team level and the organizational level. Eigel received his B.A. from Georgia State University.

George F. Farris is a professor and director of the Technology Management Research Center at Rutgers Faculty of Management. He specializes in the management of the technical workforce. Farris holds a Ph.D. from the University of Michigan.

Raghu Garud is associate professor of management at the Leonard N. Stern School of Business, New York University. His teaching and research interests are in exploring the intersection between technology, organizations, and strategy. Garud received his Ph.D. in strategic management and organization from the University of Minnesota.

Michele J. Gelfand is a visiting assistant professor in industrial/organizational psychology at New York University. She is currently doing research on the effects of individualism and collectivism on group negotiations, the advantages and disadvantages of diversity in work groups, and basic theoretical and methodological issues in cross-cultural research. Gelfand is pursuing her doctorate in social-organizational psychology from the University of Illinois, Urbana-Champaign.

Keith James is associate professor of social and organizational psychology at Colorado State University. His research and applied work deals with American-Indian education and economic issues; cultural and diversity issues in organizations; social and individual factors in creativity and innovation; workplace health and safety; and workplace technology and technology training. James holds a doctorate in social psychology and organizational behavior from the University of Arizona.

Ellen Ernst Kossek is an associate professor of human resource management/organizational behavior at Michigan State University. Her research interests are in human resource initiatives, diversity, and work and family issues. Kossek holds a Ph.D. from Yale University.

Kristine Kuhn is a doctoral student in industrial/organizational psychology at the University of Illinois, Urbana-Champaign. Her research interests include judgment and decision making, social processes in organizations, judgmental forecasting, and strategic planning.

Karl W. Kuhnert is an associate professor in the Department of Psychology at the University of Georgia. He has a special interest in leadership and change within large organizations, both for-profit and not-for-profit. Kuhnert received his doctorate in industrial/organizational psychology from Kansas State University.

Margarita C. Mayo is a doctoral candidate in organizational behavior at the School of Management, State University of New York at Buffalo. Her research interests include demographic diversity, leadership, social identity, and social networks. Mayo received an M.A. in social psychology from Clark University.

James R. Meindl is a professor of organization and director of the Center for International Leadership, School of Management, State University of New York at Buffalo. His current work focuses on the social construction of leadership and he has done work on the romance of leadership, cognition, group identity, and social justice. Meindl received his Ph.D. in social psychology from the University of Waterloo.

Juan-Carlos Pastor is a doctoral candidate in organizational behavior at the School of Management, State University of New York at Buffalo. His research interests include charismatic leadership, social networks, and the diffusion of ideologies in organizations. Pastor received an M.A. in social psychology from Clark University.

Sumita Raghuram is a visiting assistant professor at Fordham University in New York City. Her research interests include "telework" issues, workforce diversity, and strategic human resources management. She received her Ph.D. in human resource management from the University of Minnesota.

Phanikiran Radhakrishnan is a doctoral student in organizational psychology at the University of Illinois, Urbana-Champaign. Her research focuses on how cultural, informational, and motivational variables influence person perception and the impact of different types of perceptions on a variety of social and organizational outcomes, such as interpersonal interactions, performance evaluations, and psychological well-being.

Willard Young is an organizational-development consultant for Ford Motor Company. He is a graduate of the School of Labor and Industrial Relations at Michigan State University.

Susan C. Zonia is an assistant professor in the College of Osteopathic Medicine at Michigan State University. Her primary research interest is in organizational-evaluation studies. Zonia holds a Ph.D. in sociology from Michigan State University.